Photoshop 4
Type Magic 1

Photoshop 4
Type Magic 1

BY DAVID LAI AND GREG SIMSIC

Hayden
Books

Photoshop 4 Type Magic 1

Library of Congress Catalog Number: 97-071008
ISBN: 1-56830-380-7

Copyright © 1997 Hayden Books

Printed in the United States of America 1 2 3 4 5 6 7 8 9 0

Warning and Disclaimer

Trademark Acknowledgments

The Photoshop 4 Type Magic 1 Team

President
Richard Swadley

Associate Publisher
John Pierce

Publishing Manager
Laurie Petrycki

Managing Editor
Lisa Wilson

Marketing Manager
Stacey Oldham

Acquisitions Editor
Rachel Byers

Development Editors
Beth Millett

Copy/Production Editor
Kevin Laseau

Technical Editors
Kate Binder, Rick Wallace

Publishing Coordinator
Karen Flowers

Cover Designer
Aren Howell

Book Designer
Gary Adair

Manufacturing Coordinator
Brook Farling

Production Team Supervisors
Laurie Casey, Joe Millay

Production Team
Dan Caparo, Diana Groth, Mary Hunt,
Billy Huys, Pamela Woolf

Composed in *Bembo* and *GillSans*

Some thumbtab imagery provided by CMCD, Digital Stock,
D'Pix, FotoSets, Image Club Graphics, and PhotoDisc, 1997.

v

About the Authors

David Lai is the author of *Icons for the Masses* published by Peachpit Press and owner of Lai Design.

Greg Simsic, currently a student of sculpture at Herron School of Art in Indianapolis, is the author of *Photoshop Type Magic 2*, published by Hayden Books.

Hayden Books

The staff of Hayden Books is committed to bringing you the best computer books. What our readers think of Hayden is important to our ability to serve our customers. If you have any comments, no matter how great or how small, we'd appreciate your taking the time to send us a note.

You can reach Hayden Books at the following:

Hayden Books
201 West 103rd Street
Indianapolis, IN 46290
317-581-3833

Email addresses:

America Online: Hayden Bks
Internet: hayden@hayden.com

Visit the Hayden Books Web site at http://www.hayden.com

Contents

About This Book

Welcome

Welcome to this collection of special type techniques for Adobe Photoshop users. More than a how-to manual, this book is a what-to guide. The steps in this book tell you what you need to do in order to create exactly what you want. Flip through the alphabetized thumbtabs to find the type effect you want to create and follow the concise, explanatory steps. If you need a little extra help, flip to the Photoshop Basics section. But, before you jump into the type treatments, let me tell you a little about how this book works. A quick read now will maximize your time later.

System Setup

Here are the system recommendations for creating these type treatments.

Mac users: The Adobe Photoshop 4 Info box suggests a memory allocation of 21 megabytes (MB) of RAM to run Photoshop, and your system software may need as much as 10MB of RAM. That's a full bowl of soup, but if you've got the memory, then we would recommend setting the Preferred memory size even higher than 21MB. If you don't have 21MB to spare, then just quit all other applications and give it everything you've got.

PC users: Adobe suggests 32MB of RAM for Photoshop on any 386 or faster processor running Windows 3.1, Windows 95, or Windows NT, but 40MB is better. Quit any application you can before starting Photoshop to maximize the running of the application. Photoshop runs 32-bit native on both Windows 95 and Windows NT operating systems.

It is not crucial, but it will help if you have a CD-ROM drive. A number of the effects in this book use files that are contained on the CD-ROM that comes bundled with this book. (See Appendix A, "What's On the CD-ROM," for information on accessing those files.) If you don't have a CD-ROM drive, however, you still can perform all of the effects described in the book.

Adobe Photoshop 4

All of the techniques in this book were created with Adobe Photoshop 4, and that's the version we recommend you use. If you're attempting to duplicate these techniques using an earlier version of Photoshop, your results may differ slightly or significantly compared to ours. If you're working with version 3, then you still will be able to create all of the effects in the book. Keep in mind, however, that you will need to adjust the instructions for the differences between the two versions. You will see that even some of the old Photoshop features work differently in Photoshop 4. Most of the effects in this book use features that were not available in earlier versions of Photoshop.

Conventions

Every image in this book was created initially as a RGB file. You can make your effects in any appropriate color mode, but you should be aware of the variations this will cause as you proceed through the steps. The first new channel created in an RGB file, for example, is automatically named Channel #4. But the first new channel created in a CMYK file is named Channel #5. You also should be aware of the differences in the color ranges of the various color modes. Some colors that look great in RGB mode may look like mud after you convert the file color mode to CMYK. **Note:** Quite a few techniques in this book use the Lighting Effects filter. This filter will not work in a CMYK or Grayscale file.

If you'd like more detailed information about the different color modes, refer to a good general Photoshop book such as *Photoshop 4 Complete* or to your Photoshop user manuals.

Also, every type image was created as a 5×2-inch, 150-dpi resolution file. (The thumbtab images were created as 300 dpi files.) If you are going to work in a resolution other than 150 dpi, remember that some of the filters and commands will require different settings than the settings I used. Because there are fewer pixels in a 72 dpi image, a Gaussian Blur radius of 5 pixels blurs the image more than if it were a 150 dpi image. Just keep an eye on the figures next to the steps and match the outcome as closely as you can.

The Toolbox

For some of the effects, I used a third-party filter or a specially prepared preset file. Any of these extra tools that are not included with the standard Photoshop software are listed in the Toolbox in the lower-left corner of the first page of each technique. The Toolbox lists everything that you'll need to create each type effect and any of its variations. The CD-ROM that comes with this book contains all of the files needed to perform all of the basic techniques. For information on accessing and installing these files, turn to Appendix A, "What's On the CD-ROM."

The Blue Type

As you work through the steps, you will see phrases colored blue. These same phrases are listed in alphabetical order in the Photoshop Basics section (pages 5–21). If the phrase in blue asks you to perform a task unfamiliar to you, then you can find that phrase in the Photoshop Basics section and follow the instructions on how to perform that task.

2

Menu Commands

You also will see instructions that look like this:

Filter➡Blur➡Gaussian Blur (2 pixels)

This example asks you to apply the Gaussian Blur filter. To perform this command, click the Filter menu at the top of the screen and drag down to Blur. When Blur is highlighted a new menu opens to the right, from which you can choose Gaussian Blur.

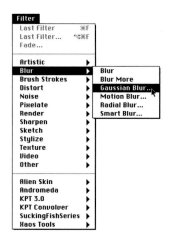

In this example, a dialog box appears asking you for more information. All of the settings that you need to perform each task appear in the text of the step. The previous example tells you to enter 2 pixels as the Radius.

Click OK to blur the type.

3

Settings

Following each action in the steps, you will find the settings for that feature. These recommended settings are meant to act as guides; the best settings for your type effect may vary depending on variables such as your font, color, background, or size. As a rule of thumb, it is best to match the outcomes that you see in the figures as you progress through the technique. The greatest differences occur when the resolution of your file or the point size of your type are significantly different from what we used. The following two images demonstrate the importance of adjusting for resolution differences. A 6-pixel Radius Gaussian Blur was applied to both images.

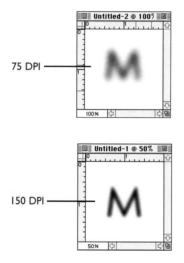

Tips

Throughout the book, you will find additional bits of information that can help you render a better type effect. These tips provide information beyond the basic steps of each lesson. ■

4

Photoshop Basics

The goal of this section is to help novice users of Photoshop with the simple, basic tasks required to create the type effects described and illustrated in this book. Each of the basic tasks described in this section corresponds to the blue text in the chapters that follow. Here, users can easily find the instructions they need for performing a particular Photoshop task.

This chapter proceeds on two assumptions: that you're creating our type effects in Photoshop 4; and that you're keeping the Tool and Layer/Channel/Path palettes open. If one or both of the Tool and Layer/Channel/Path palettes are closed when you refer to this chapter, you can reopen them by name by using the Window menu at the top of the screen. If you're using an earlier version of Photoshop, you can refer to the Photoshop manual for instructions on how to perform these tasks. Also, keep in mind that Photoshop 2.5 does not offer the capability to work in layers.

The Toolbox

If you're not familiar with Photoshop's Toolbox, there's no reason to panic. With a bit of experimentation, it doesn't take long to learn each tool's individual functions. To help the beginning Photoshop user along the way, here is a representation of the toolbars from both Photoshop 3 and 4. This will also help advanced users find the rearranged tools.

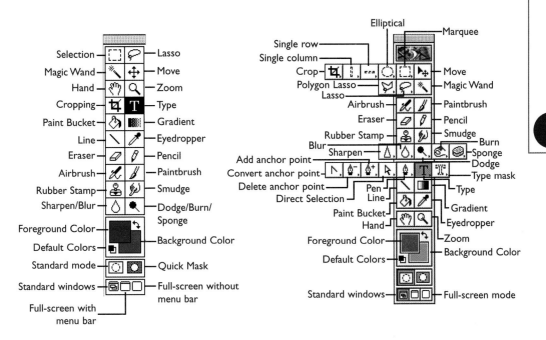

Choose a Foreground or Background Color

Shortcut: Press D to change colors to their defaults: black for the foreground, and white for the background if you're working on a layer, and the other way around in a channel or on a layer mask or adjustment layer.

Press X to switch the foreground color with the the background color.

To change the foreground or background color click either the Foreground icon or the Background icon.

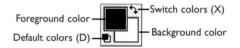

Foreground color ⎯ Switch colors (X)

Default colors (D) ⎯ Background color

The Color Picker dialog box appears, which enables you to choose a new foreground or background color by moving and clicking the cursor (now a circle) along the spectrum box, or by changing specific RGB, CMYK, or other percentage values. Note that the Foreground and Background color icons on the Toolbox now reflect your color choices.

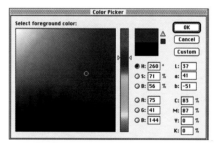

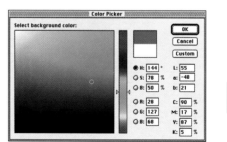

Convert to a New Mode

To convert from one color mode to another, click the Image menu at the top of the screen and scroll down to the Mode selection. You then can scroll down to select the mode of your preference. If, for example, you want to switch from CMYK mode to Multichannel mode, you choose Image➡Mode➡Multichannel. The check mark to the left of CMYK moves down to Multichannel, indicating that you are now in Multichannel mode.

TIP Remember that there is a different range of colors available for each color mode. **No matter what color mode the file is in onscreen, for example, your printer (if it prints in color) is going to print your work in CMYK. Because the color ranges for RGB and CMYK are different, you should convert your RGB image to CMYK before printing. Otherwise, you may be in for a big surprise when your bright green prints as a dull tan.**

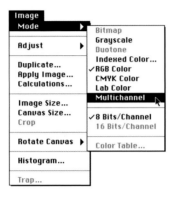

Create a Layer Mask

Shortcuts: Click the Add Layer Mask icon on the Layers palette.

To create a layer mask, choose Layer➡Add Layer Mask, and choose either Reveal All (white) or Hide All (black). For the purposes of the effects in this book, always choose Reveal All. A layer mask is used to mask out (or hide) specified parts of a layer.

7

Create a New Channel

Shortcuts: Click the New Channel icon on the Channels palette.

To create a new channel, choose New Channel from the Channels palette pop-up menu.

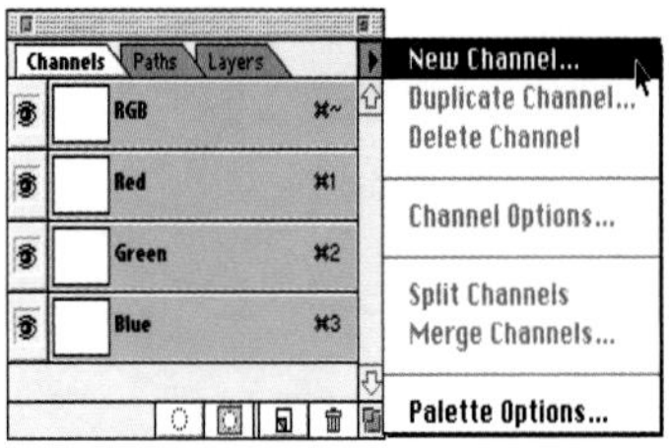

Use the Channel Options dialog box to establish your settings. Unless noted otherwise, we used the default settings when creating a new channel. This figure shows Photoshop's default settings.

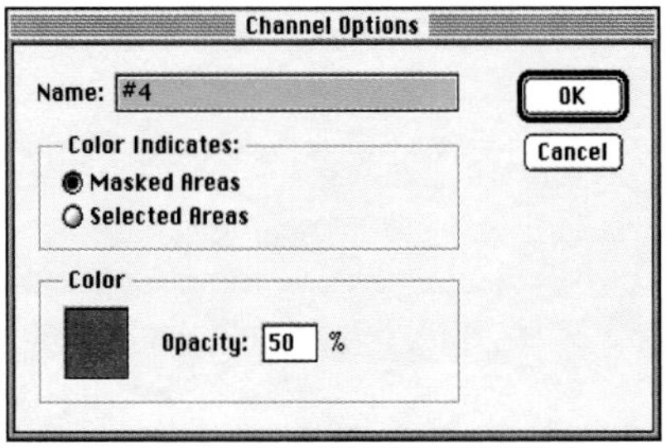

Create a New File

Shortcuts: Press (Command-N) [Control-N].

To create a new file, choose File➡New. The New dialog box appears, which is where you name your new file and establish other settings. See "About This Book" for information on the conventions that were used when creating new files for the type effects in this book.

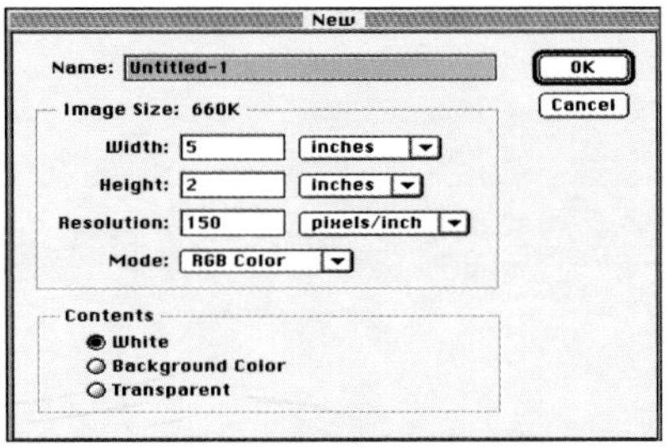

8

Create a New Layer

Shortcuts: Click the New Layer icon on the Layers palette.

To create a new layer, choose New Layer from the Layer palette pop-up menu, or choose Layer➡New➡Layer.

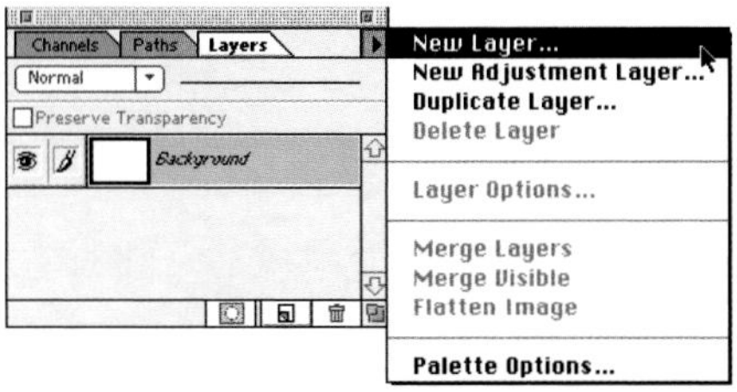

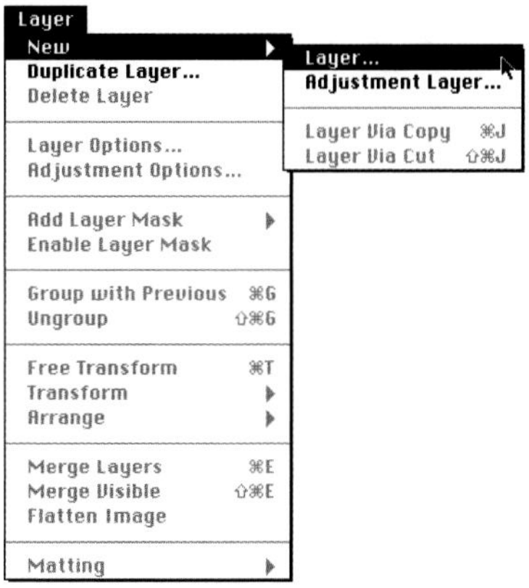

The New Layer dialog box opens, which is where you name the new layer and establish other settings.

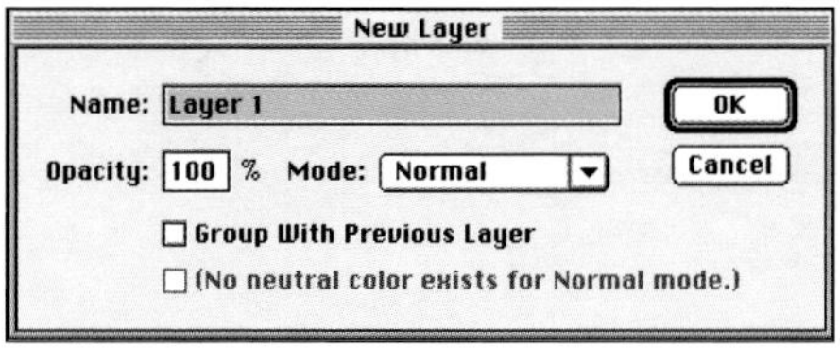

9

Delete a Channel

To delete a channel, go to the Channels palette and select the channel you want to delete; drag it to the Trash icon at the lower-right corner. You also can select the channel you want to delete, and choose Delete Channel from the Channels palette menu.

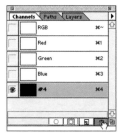

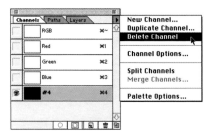

Deselect a Selection

Shortcut: Press (Command-D) [Control]-D.

To deselect a selection, choose Select➡None. The marquee disappears.

Duplicate a Channel

Shortcut: Click the channel you want to duplicate, and drag it on top of the New Channel icon.

To create a duplicate of a channel, make the channel active and then select Duplicate Channel from the Channels palette menu.

A new copy of the channel you selected for duplication is created automatically, and the Duplicate Channel dialog box appears.

Enter/Exit Quick Mask

Shortcuts: Press Q to enter and exit the Quick Mask mode.

Click the Quick Mask icon to switch to Quick Mask mode; conversely, click the Standard mode icon to return to Standard mode.

Essentially a Quick Mask is a temporary channel. When you're in Quick Mask mode you can use any of the Photoshop tools and functions to change the selection without changing the image. When you switch back to Standard mode you'll have a new selection.

Enter the Text

There are two type tools in Photoshop 4; the standard Type tool and the Type Mask tool. Each effect in this book specifies which type tool to use.

Before entering the text using the standard Type tool, make sure that the foreground color is set to your desired text color. Often, the instructions in this book ask you to enter text into a channel. Unless noted otherwise, it is assumed that you are entering white text onto the black background of the channel. If you are entering text into a layer, then the standard Type tool creates a new layer for the type.

The Type Mask tool creates selection outlines of the text you enter without filling the outlines with a new color, and without creating a new layer.

To enter the text, select the type tool that you want to use, and then click anywhere in the image to open the Type Tool dialog box. Type the text in the large box at the bottom of the dialog box, and make your attribute choices from the options (listed previously). Unless noted otherwise in the instructions, always make sure that you have the Anti-Aliased box checked.

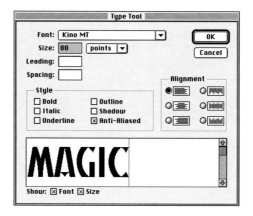

After clicking OK, move the type into position with the Move tool (if you entered your text with the standard Type tool) or Marquee tool (if you used the Type Mask tool).

Fill a Selection with Foreground or Background Color

First, select the foreground or background color you want to use (see page 6 in this section for instructions). Keep the selection active and press the (Option-Delete) [Alt-Delete] keys to fill the selection with the foreground color. If you are in the Background layer or any layer that has the Preserve Transparency option turned on, then you can press Delete to fill in the selection with the background color.

You also can fill in your selections by choosing Edit➡Fill, or press (Shift-Delete) [Shift-Backspace] to bring up the Fill dialog box.

This causes the Fill dialog box to appear, enabling you to establish the Contents option you want to use, the Opacity, and the Blending Mode.

TIP If a selection is empty (a transparent area of a layer) and the **Preserve Transparency** option is turned on for that layer, then you will not be able to fill the selection. To fill the selection, simply turn off the Preserve Transparency option before filling it.

Flatten an Image

13

To flatten an image (merge all the layers into a single layer), choose Flatten Image from the Layers palette menu, or choose Layer➡Flatten Image.

Load a Selection

Shortcut: Hold down the (Command) [Control] key and click the channel (on the Channels palette) that contains the selection you want to load.

To load a selection, choose Select➥Load Selection. This brings up the Load Selection dialog box, where you can establish document, channel, and operation variables.

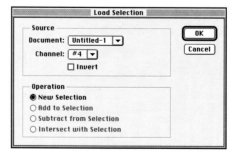

Load the Transparency Mask (of a Layer)

To load the transparency selection of a layer, hold down the (Command) [Control] key and click the layer (on the Layers palette) that contains the transparency selection you want to load.

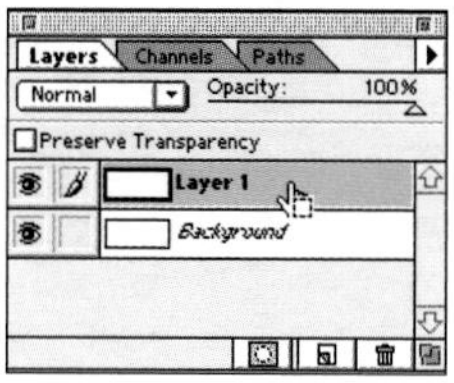

Make a Channel Active

To make a channel active for editing or modification, click its thumbnail or title on the Channels palette.

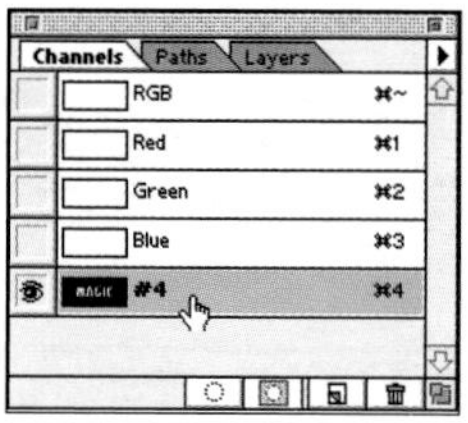

You can tell the channel is active if it is highlighted with a color.

Make a Layer Active

To make a layer active, click its thumbnail or title in the Layers palette.

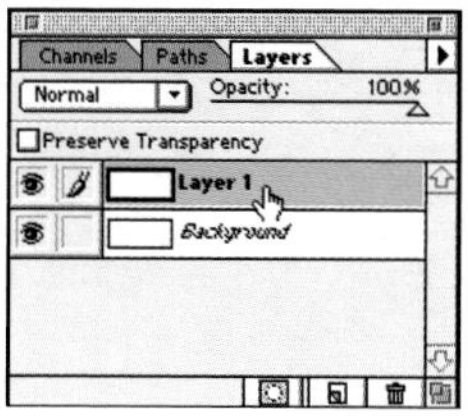

You can tell the layer is active if it is highlighted with a color.

15

Make a Layer Visible/Invisible

To make a layer visible, click in the left-most column in the Layers palette. If the Eye icon appears, then the layer is visible. If the column is empty, then that layer is hidden (invisible).

Move a Layer

To change the stacking order of a layer, click the layer you want to move in the Layers palette and drag it up or down the list of layers to the place you want to move it. As you drag the layer, the lines between the layers darken to indicate where the layer will fall if you let go.

The layer you moved appears between layers.

Rename a Layer or Channel

Shortcuts: Double-click the layer or channel name to bring up the options dialog box. You can change the name in this dialog box.

To rename a layer or channel, chose Layer Options or Channel Options from the Layer or Channel palette's pop-up menu. This will bring up an options dialog box where you can edit the name.

Return to the Composite Channel

Shortcut: Press (Command-~) [Control-~].

If you want to return to the composite channel, click its thumbnail or title (RGB, CMYK, Lab). The composite channel will always be the one with (Command-~) [Control-~] after its title.

17

If you are in an RGB file, then Channels 0 through 3 should now be active because each of the R, G, and B channels are individual parts of the RGB channel.

Save a File

Shortcut: Press (Shift-Command-S) [Shift-Control-S] to bring up the Save As dialog box.

To save a file, choose File➡Save As. This displays the Save As dialog box, where you name your new file and choose a format in which to save it.

File format selection depends on what you have in your file, what you want to keep when you save it, and what you're going to do with the file after it is saved. Consult a detailed Photoshop book, such as *Photoshop 4 Complete*, for more guidance on which file format is best for your needs.

File	
New...	⌘N
Open...	▶
Close	⌘W
Save	⌘S
Save As...	⇧⌘S
Save a Copy...	⌥⌘S
Revert	
Place...	▶
Import	▶
Export	▶
File Info...	
Page Setup...	⇧⌘P
Print...	⌘P
Preferences	▶
Color Settings	▶
Quit	⌘Q

Folder File Drive Options

🔲 Save Here ▼   ⊃Where?

Eject

Desktop

New 🗀

Save this document as: Cancel

Untitled-1   Save

Format: TIFF ▼

Save a Selection

Shortcut: Click the Save Selection icon on the Channels palette.

To save a selection, choose Select➡Save Selection.

18

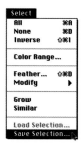

The Save Selection dialog box opens. Choose your options and click OK to save the selection.

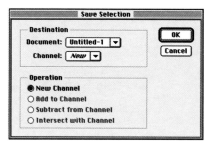

Switch Foreground/Background Colors

Shortcut: Press X to switch the foreground and background colors.

To switch the foreground and background colors, click the Switch Colors icon. This flips the two colors shown in this icon only, and does not affect the rest of the image.

Switch colors

Switch to Default Colors

Shortcut: Press D to switch to the default foreground and background colors.

To change the foreground and background colors to black and white respectively (if you're on a layer), click the Default Colors icon. If you're working in a channel or on a layer mask or adjustment layer, clicking the Default Colors icon changes the foreground colors to white and black, respectively.

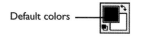

Default colors

Turn On/Off Preserve Transparency

To turn on or off the Preserve Transparency option for a particular layer, first make that layer the active layer. Then, click the Preserve Transparency checkbox on the Layers palette. This option is not available for the Background layer. ■

These steps provide some tips and tricks on how to work through the assembly process. Remember, though, that every assemblage project is going to present its own problems that require unique solutions.

1 Create a new file. Use the Type tool to enter the text that serves as a guide for the assembled type. I used a simple sans serif font, Helvetica, at 125 point with a spacing of 5 between the letters. This gave us more room to work. Note that Photoshop 4.0 creates a new layer with the type on it. Name this layer "Guide."

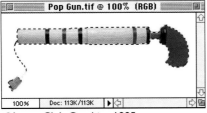

©Image Club Graphics 1995

2 Next, open the file containing the art you are using to assemble the type. I opened a stock photo from Image Club Graphics. Use the Selection tools to select the item you want to use for assembling the type. Linear shapes are obviously the easiest to work with when creating type. Draw a path around irregular shapes and then convert it into a selection. After selecting the item, copy it to the clipboard (Command-C) [Control-C].

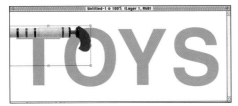

3 Return to your text file and paste from the clipboard (Command-V) [Control-V]. Again, Photoshop 4.0 automatically places the item in a new layer. I moved and scaled the pop gun (Layer➡Transform➡Scale) into position as the horizontal member of the letter T.

Then use the selection tools to crop the T. Remember to use the background type as your guide.

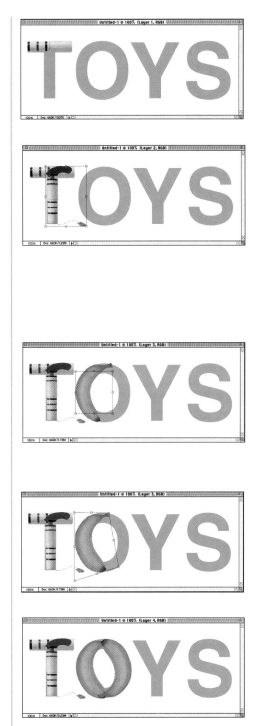

4 To make the vertical component of the T, paste the picture of the pop gun from the clipboard again (Command-V) [Control-V]. If you haven't already noticed, every time you paste in a new item, Photoshop 4.0 places it in a new layer. Rotate (Layer➡Transform➡Rotate 90° CCW), scale (Layer➡Transform➡Scale), and move (use the Move tool) the pop gun into position to finish the T.

5 I then opened an image of a banana and copied it into the clipboard (Command-C) [Control-C]. Return to your working file and paste it from the clipboard (Command-V) [Control-V]. Then move and scale the banana (Layer➡Transform➡Scale) into position.

Then distort the banana (Layer➡Transform➡Distort) for a better fit.

6 To complete the other side of the letter O, load the selection and copy it to the clipboard (Command-C) [Control-C]. Paste in the image (Command-V) [Control-V] and rotate the banana (Layer➡Transform➡Rotate 180°). Use the Move tool to position the banana into place.

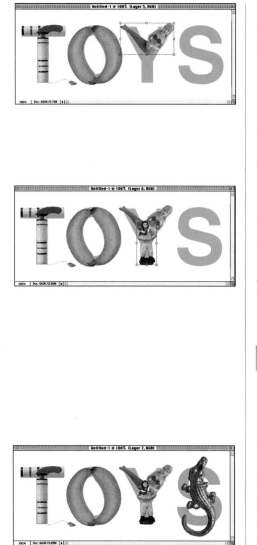

7 Look for images that most closely resemble parts of the letter you are trying to create. I copied an image of a mermaid into the clipboard (Command-C) [Control-C]. Return to your working file and paste it from the clipboard (Command-V) [Control-V]. Then move and scale the mermaid (Layer➨Transform➨Scale) over the upper portion of the Y.

8 To complete the Y, I used an image of an aviator that was opened and copied into the clipboard (Command-C) [Control-C]. Paste it from the clipboard (Command-V)[Control-V] into your file. Then move and scale it (Layer➨Transform➨Scale) into position.

TIP **Press the V key to quickly activate the Move tool. Use the arrow keys for precise control when aligning your images.**

9 Next I opened and copied an image of an alligator into the clipboard (Command-C) [Control-C]. Again, note how I chose an object that most closely represented the shape of the S. Paste it from the clipboard (Command-V) [Control-V] into your file. Then move it over the S with the Move tool.

10 Unfortunately, the shape of the alligator is not close enough to an S, so you need to use the Shear filter to help. Choose Filter➡ Distort➡ Shear. You have to adjust the settings to get the shape closest to an S.

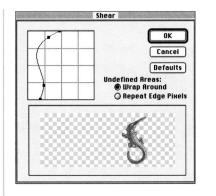

You should get something that looks like this.

11 Now you need to distort the alligator some more (Layer➡ Transform➡Distort). The guide is there to help you, but it is not critical that you follow it exactly. In this case, it is still pretty obvious that the alligator forms an S.

TIP **Use the Smudge tool to help you when you need to quickly blend together two objects. This is especially useful if you are working with organic shapes.**

12 To finalize the image, I deleted the Guide layer and flattened the image. That's all there is to it! ▦

Photo credits for this chapter: Image Club Graphics, PhotoDisc, CMCD, D'Pix, Digital Stock, 1995.

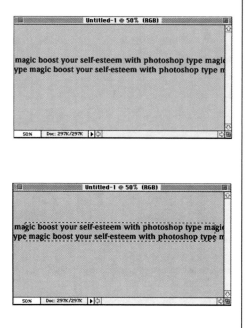

Need some cheap subliminal advertising? Here are two quick ways to create a background filled with text.

I Create a new file with the dimensions of the background you want to fill. Use the Type tool to enter the text you want repeated in the background. In the Type dialog box, type the text twice in the same row. We used Weideman Black at 17 points. After setting the type, we copied it, pasted it, and then offset the second copy. Flatten the image.

2 This is the most difficult step for this technique. You have to be careful what you select if you want to get the pattern to repeat correctly. Use the rectangular Marquee tool to draw a box around the portion of the text used as a pattern for the entire background. It's okay to cut the selection through the middle of a letter as long as the other end of the selection cuts through the same letter in the same place. You can control the spacing between lines in the final pattern by including more or less space in the selection rectangle above or below the text.

TIP Make the area you want to use for your pattern as large on the screen as you can. You can zoom in by holding down the (Command) [Control] key and Spacebar and clicking in the image, no matter which tool is currently active. To zoom back out, click within the image while holding down the (Option) [Alt] key and Spacebar.

26

3 Now choose Edit➡Define Pattern. Then Select➡All (Command-A) [Control-A] and choose Edit➡Fill (Pattern, Opacity: 100%, Normal).

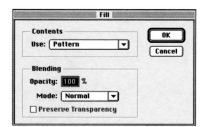

You now have a very simple background and can work on the rest of the image by creating new layers above it. Or try the following variations.

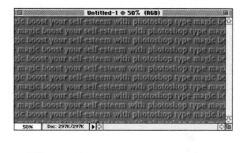

VARIATIONS

Apply Photoshop's Emboss filter…

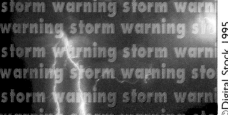

…or maybe use the Offset filter on one channel and then combine it with a photograph, such as this one from Digital Stock…

27

©Digital Stock 1995

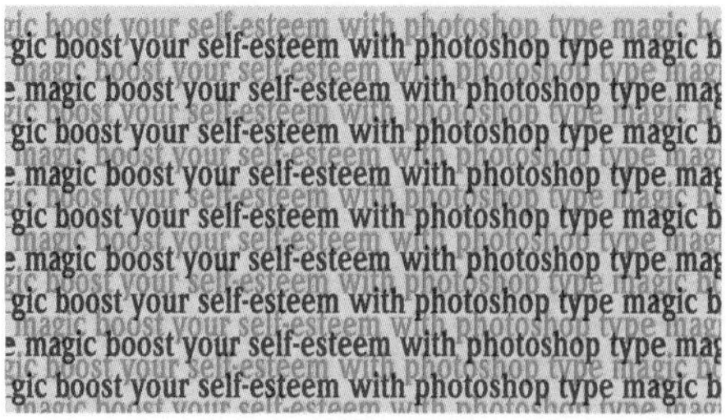

...or maybe apply the Offset filter to only one channel...

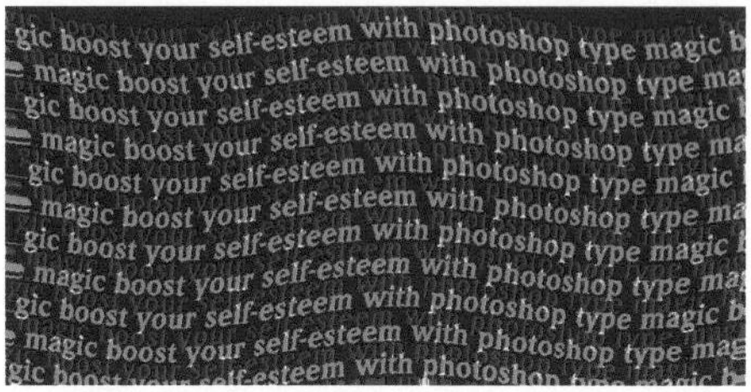

...then add the Wave filter...

...then apply the Shear filter to only one channel.

Background 2

Another way to create a background filled with text is to use the Wave filter.

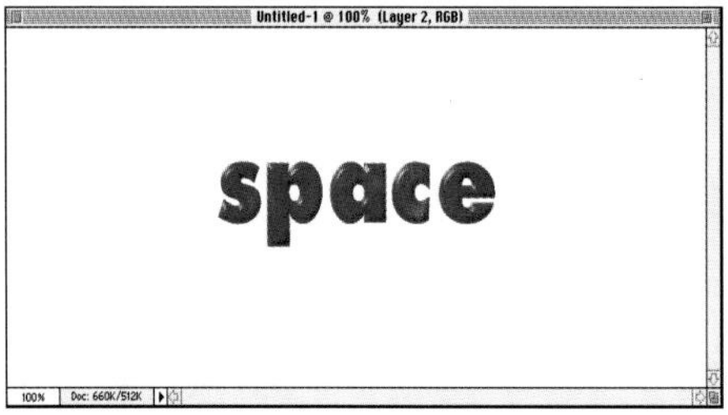

1 In a separate file create the type you want to use for the background tile. Select the text with the rectangular Marquee and copy it to the clipboard (Command-C) [Control-C].

2 Now, create a new file with the dimensions of the background you want to fill. Paste the text from the first file into this background file (Command-V) [Control-V]. Place the text in the middle of the background image.

Untitled-1 @ 100% (Layer 2, RGB)

space

100%   Doc: 660K/512K

3 Choose Filter➡Distort➡Wave. Start with these values: Generators: 5; Wavelength: 500 & 660; Amplitude: 10 & 925; Horizontal: 100%; Vertical: 100%. Choose the Wrap Around option. Of course, this is only one of the countless possibilities for this filter. Use the Randomize button to see other options, or adjust the sliders until you see something you like. You could also apply the filter again for more variations. Simply choose Filter➡Wave (Command-F) [Control-F]. Here are some of the variations we came up with. ∎

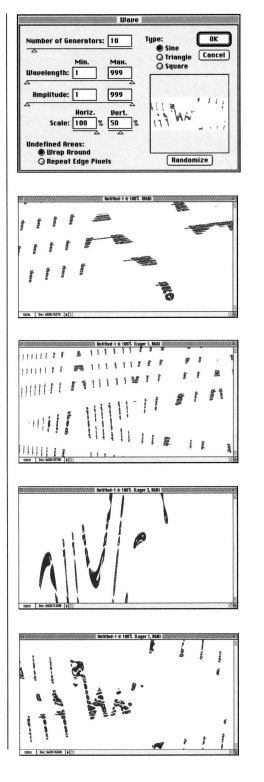

Sometimes it's best to let Adobe's other software do some of the dirty work for you—and if it's beveled text you're looking for, then Adobe Dimensions gets the honor. A demo version of Dimensions 2.0 (Mac only) is included on the CD-ROM so you can try it for yourself. If you don't have Dimensions, skip to the Photoshop Bevel section, where you can learn how to create a bevel with Photoshop's Lighting Effects filter.

Dimensions Bevel

1 Open Adobe Dimensions 2.0. A new document window automatically opens. Press (Command-E) to make sure that you are working in Edit Mode, where everything runs faster. Then choose Operations➡ Extrude (Command-Shift-E). The Extrude floating palette appears onscreen. Click the New Base button on the palette.

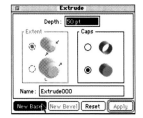

2 A new untitled window opens, and the icons in the toolbar change. Double-click the Type tool to select it and open the Character floating palette. Make your selections in the Character palette. We used 70-point Copperplate 32BC.

3 With the Type tool, click in the Extrude window that opened in Step 2. Type in the text. If you plan on having the bevels extend outward from the text, then make sure you increase the letter spacing by entering a positive value in the Tracking box. This gives them some room to spread. First, select the text by dragging the Type tool insertion bar over it. We set the tracking at 150.

TOOLBOX

Adobe Dimensions
(Mac only)

Alien Skin's Inner
Bevel filter

Alien Skin's Outer
Bevel filter

If you don't like what you see, make changes to the text by selecting the text as described earlier and making new selections in the Character palette. The text changes automatically.

4 Now click the New Bevel button on the Extrude floating palette. Move through the directories to locate the Bevel Library within the Adobe Dimensions 2.0 folder on your hard drive. Adobe provides 22 preset bevels for you to use. We chose the Classic Normal bevel. Watch the preview window and click Import when you're done.

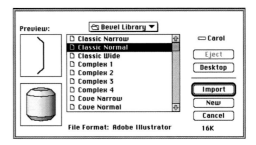

5 Another new window opens showing the contour of the bevel. Find the Extrude floating palette again. Enter, in points, the depth you want the text to extrude. Our text is going to be facing front so we entered an arbitrary medium depth of 20 points. We also chose an outer bevel and end caps.

Click the Apply button on the Extrude floating palette.

6 If you can't see the original window that opened when you opened Dimensions, choose Window➡ Untitled-1. Now you can see that the text has been extruded and beveled.

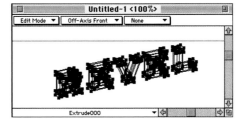

31

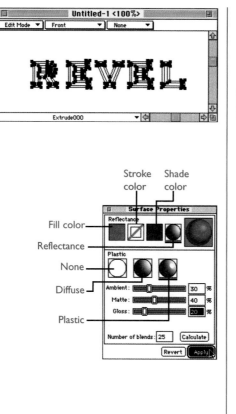

Stroke color   Shade color

Fill color
Reflectance
None
Diffuse
Plastic

7 Choose View➤View Angles➤ Front. Now, all you need to do is edit the surface properties of the text and render it.

> **TIP** **If you want to change the direction of the light source, choose Appearance ➤Lighting, and make your selections in the Lighting floating palette.**

8 Choose Appearance➤Surface Properties. A floating palette appears. The figure here explains its features. For the Fill (text) color, we used these CMYK values: 0/100/100/0. For the Shade (shadow) color, CMYK: 100/100/0/60. We left the Stroke (edge) color at none. Click the Reflectance icon, then the Plastic icon, and use the values shown in the figure. Click the Apply button when you're finished.

> **TIP** **Make sure that the number of blends is at least 25 to avoid banding. If your text has a lot of curves, you probably want to increase it.**

9 You won't see any changes in the text because you're not in a render mode yet. Choose View➤Shaded Render. (Complex text may take some time to render. Be patient.) If you don't like what you see, use the Surface Properties palette to make appearance changes or go back to the Extrude palette and use the Edit buttons to alter the text.

10 When you're satisfied, deselect the type (Command-Shift-A) [Control-Shift-A], and choose File➥Export. In the Export dialog box, choose Color Macintosh and Adobe Illustrator from the pop-up menus. Quit Dimensions (Command-Q) [Control-Q].
No need to save changes—you already exported what you wanted.

11 Open Photoshop, and open the file you just exported from Adobe Dimensions. Here are the settings we used in the Rasterize box:

12 The text opens into Layer 1 and there is no background layer.

13 If you simply want a white background, choose Flatten Image from the Layers palette menu. If not, take a look at the Variations section.

VARIATIONS

If you want to make modifications to the text, don't flatten the image. (Command-clicking) [Control-clicking] the layer in the Layers palette selects the text. Now you can use any of Photoshop's tools to alter the text.

33

To change the color of the text, choose Image➤Adjust➤Hue/Saturation, check the Colorize option, and use the Hue slider to find or modify the color.

To add a background, create a new layer (Layer 2), and move the layer in the Layers palette below Layer 1. The new layer is the active one. Fill the background with a color or paste in an image.

To get this transparent bevel, we put the same beveled text on a background and double-clicked Layer 1 (the beveled text layer) in the Layers palette to bring up the Layers Options dialog box. The settings we used are shown in this figure.

For this variation we used KPT 3 Gradient Designer to fill the selection with the Metal Sweep Cymbal II + a gradient. We chose Procedural Blend from the Options menu. After applying the blend, we raised the contrast using the Levels (Command-L) [Control-L] dialog box.

Photoshop Bevel

1 Create a new file (it must be in RGB mode). Create a new channel (#4), and use the Type tool to enter the text. We used Frutiger Bold at 70 points.

2 Duplicate Channel #4 to create Channel #5. Deselect the text (Command-D) [Control-D]. Choose Filter➟Blur➟Gaussian blur (5 pixels). The blurring creates the area for the bevel.

3 Load the original text channel selection (#4). Choose Select➟ Modify➟Contract (3 pixels). Fill the selection with white so the bevel has hard edges.

4 Return to the composite channel. Load the selection Channel #4. Fill the selection with a color for the type.

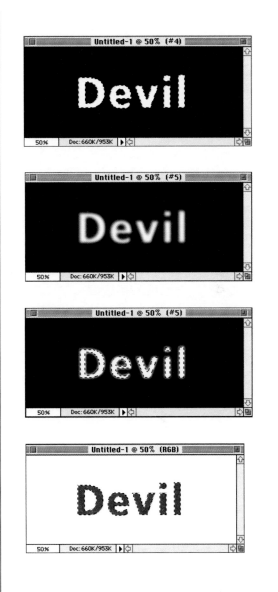

Beveled

36

Lighting Effects

Style: BevelLightStyles

Save... Delete

OK

Cancel

Light Type: Omni

☒ On

Intensity: Negative 32 Full

Focus: Narrow 69 Wide

Properties

Gloss: Matte 20 Shiny

Material: Plastic 100 Metallic

Exposure: Under 0 Over

Ambience: Negative 10 Positive

Texture Channel: #5

☒ White is high

Height: Flat 50 Mountainous

☒ Preview

Devil

Untitled-1 @ 100% (RGB)

Devil

50% Doc: 660K/953K

Devil

5 Choose Filter➡Render➡Lighting Effects. From the pop-up menu choose BevelLightStyles, or match the settings shown in this figure. Make sure you specify the Texture Channel (#5) when you apply this filter.

Click OK and you've got beveled text.

MORE VARIATIONS

To bevel a surface, before Step 1 copy the surface into the clipboard. Then, in Step 4, instead of filling the text with a color, choose Edit➡ Paste Into. Also, to automatically add a drop shadow we chose Select➡None at the end of Step 4.

Alien Skin's Outer Bevel 2.0 and Inner Bevel 2.0 filters make beveling a breeze. If you use the outer bevel, remember that the filter uses the color outside the text selection for the color of the beveled edges. If you want the bevels to be the same color as the text then the text should be placed on a background of the same color. For this variation, we placed white text on a stock photo from PhotoDisc. ▪

©PhotoDisc 1995

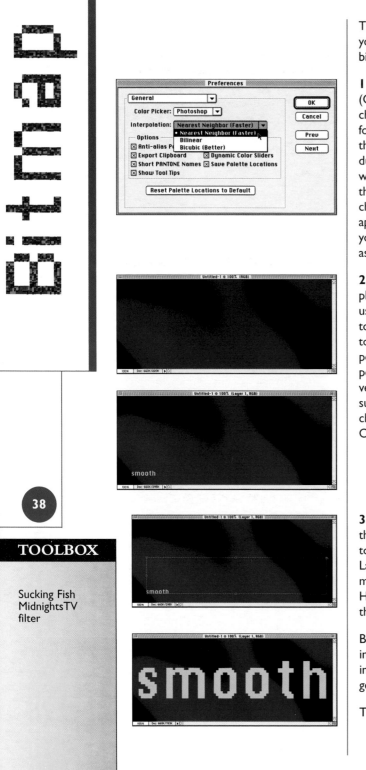

Bitmap

This technique is especially useful if you are trying to quickly get the bitmapped, computer look.

1 In the File➡Preferences➡General (Command-K) [Control-K] menu, choose Nearest Neighbor (Faster) for the Interpolation Method. When this method is used, Photoshop duplicates the neighboring pixels when a selection is enlarged rather than averaging them. Remember to change your preferences back after applying this technique; otherwise you'll start seeing all your graphics as big, blocky bitmaps.

2 Create a new file. In this example, we created a background first using a KPT filter. Choose the Type tool and enter the text. In the Type tool dialog box, choose a small point size. We used Chicago at 10 points. This enables your text to be very bitmapped when enlarged. Be sure that Anti-Aliased is not checked. Type your text and click OK.

3 (Command-click) [Control-click] the type layer in the Layers palette to select the type, and choose Layer➡Transform➡Scale from the menu bar and enlarge the text. Holding down the Shift key keeps the selection in proportion.

Because the Nearest Neighbor interpolation method was chosen in Step 1, the enlarged selection gets blocky.

That's all there is to it!

38

Sucking Fish
Midnights TV
filter

VARIATIONS

Add smooth text to contrast the "jaggies" for a nice effect.

You can get an outline around your text by using Edit➡Stroke. This command strokes the selection with the foreground color, so be sure it's not the same color as your text!

After enlarging the text a little (about 25%), choose Filter➡ Noise➡Add Noise. Then enlarge the text even more. The noisy pixels inside the text enlarge along with the text, complementing the bitmappy look.

Or, instead of using Filter➡Noise, try Filter➡MidnightsTV (from the Sucking Fish Series of filters). ■

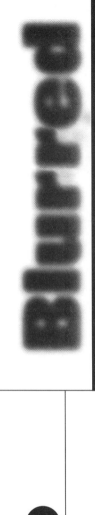

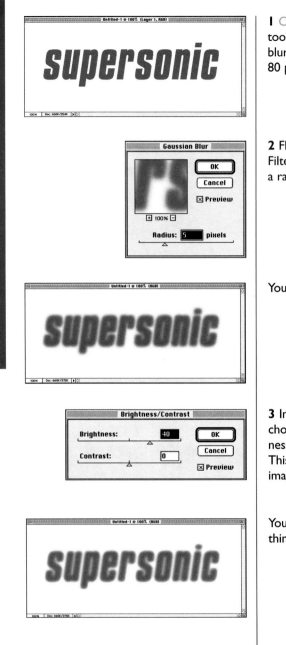

1 Create a new file. Use the Type tool to enter the text you want to blur. I used Compact Bold Italic at 80 points in this example.

2 Flatten the image. Then apply Filter→Blur→Gaussian Blur. I used a radius of 5 pixels.

You should get something like this.

3 In order to lighten the type, choose Image→Adjust→ Brightness/Contrast (Brightness: +40). This adds some haziness to the image.

Your type should now look something like this.

40

VARIATIONS

Blurred text looks particularly good when contrasted against unblurred text.

After applying Photoshop's Gaussian Blur filter, choose Filter➡Other➡Minimum to beef up the blur. The higher the setting, the wider the blur. A setting of 5 pixels was used here.

The result is a more robust blur.

You could also use Filter➡Other➡ Maximum to thin down the type. A setting of 7 pixels was used here.

Some interesting residue is left between the letters.

41

Clouds

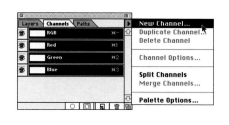

1 Create a new file, and create a new channel (Channel #4).

2 Set the foreground color to white. Enter your text into Channel #4. A round-edged font such as VAG Rounded, which I used here at 80 points, works best.

TIP **Try using a script font such as Brush Script for sky writing effects!**

3 Return to the composite channel (Command-~) [Control-~] and Select➡All. Change the background color to a sky blue. Select Filter➡Render➡Clouds.

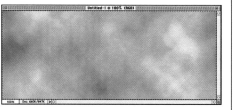

4 Load the selection Channel #4.

5 Now choose Select➡Feather and use a setting of 7 pixels.

TIP **If you increase the Feather settings, you increase the radius of the feather. Similarly, by decreasing the settings, you decrease the radius of the feather.**

6 Press (Option-Delete) [Alt-Delete] to fill the selection with white. ■

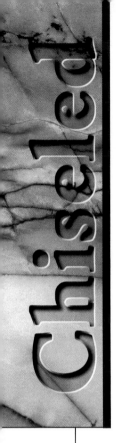

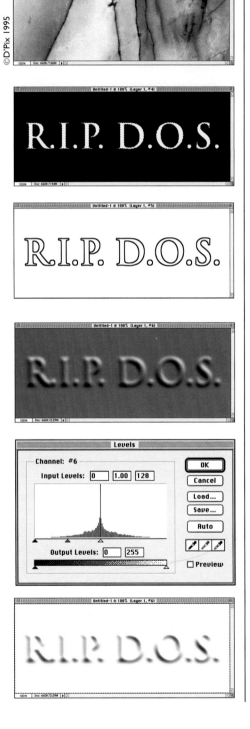

1 Open a file containing the background you want to chisel. Obviously, a marble or stone texture works best for this effect. We used a stock photo of a piece of rosetta marble from D'Pix for this example.

2 Create a new channel (Channel #4), and change the foreground color to white. Use the Type tool to enter the text in the new channel. This epitaph appears in Trajan Bold at 55 points.

3 Create another new channel (Channel #5). Choose Edit➡Stroke (3 pixels, Outside, 100%, Normal). Choose Select➡None (Command-D) [Control-D] and Image➡Adjust➡Invert (Command-I) [Control-I].

4 Make Channel #4 active and duplicate it to create Channel #6. Choose Filter➡Blur➡Gaussian Blur (6 pixels). Choose Filter➡Stylize➡Emboss (240°, 3 pixels, 200%).

5 Select➡All (Command-A) [Control-A] and Copy (Command-C) [Control-C] the image to the clipboard. Choose Image➡Adjust➡Levels (Input Levels: 0, 1, 128).

6 Load the selection Channel #5. Press (Option-Delete) [Alt-Delete] to fill the background with white. Deselect the text. Choose Image➡ Adjust➡Invert (Command-I) [Control-I].

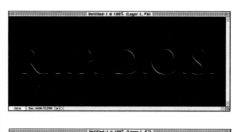

7 Create a new channel (#7) and paste (Command-V) [Control-V] in the clipboard. Choose Image➡ Adjust➡Invert (Command-I) [Control-I], then Image➡Adjust ➡Levels (Input Levels: 0, 1, 128).

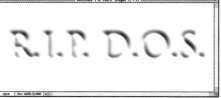

8 Load the selection Channel #5. Press (Option-Delete) [Alt-Delete] to fill the background with white. Deselect the text. Choose Image➡ Adjust➡Invert (Command-I) [Control-I].

9 Make Channel #4 active and duplicate it to create Channel #8. Choose Image➡Adjust➡Invert (Command-I) [Control-I]. Apply Filter➡Blur➡Gaussian Blur (3 pixels). Change the background color to white. Select➡All (Command-A) [Control-A] and press the left arrow key and down arrow key four times to offset the image.

10 Load the selection Channel #4. Choose Select➡Inverse. Change the foreground color to black and press (Option-Delete) [Alt-Delete] to fill the selection.

45

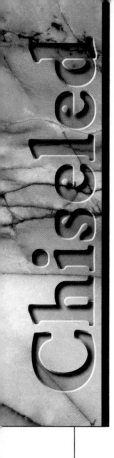

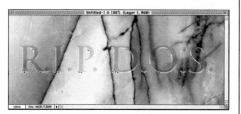

11 Return to the composite channel. Make sure the foreground color is black. Choose Select➡Load Selection (Channel #4) and Edit➡Fill (Foreground Color, 15%, Normal).

12 Load the selection Channel #6 and change the foreground color to white. Press (Option-Delete) [Alt-Delete] twice to fill the selection twice.

13 Load the selection Channel #7 and change the foreground color to black. Press (Option-Delete) [Alt-Delete] twice to fill the selection twice.

14 Load the selection Channel #8 then Edit➡Fill (Foreground Color, 85%, Normal). You might want to make adjustments to the Opacity setting to get the desired effect since this may vary from image to image. ∎

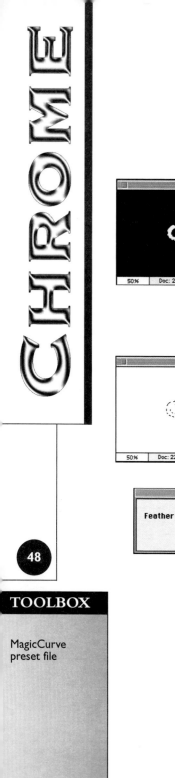

TOOLBOX

MagicCurve
preset file

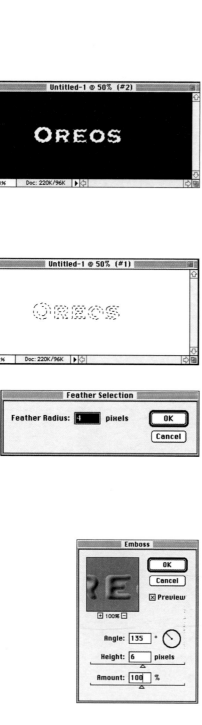

1 Create a new file, selecting the Grayscale mode in the New File dialog box. In the new file, choose Mode➡Multichannel. Create a new channel (#2). You should now see a blank, black image area.

2 Make sure that the foreground color is white. Click the Type tool, choose the font you wish to use (in this example, we used Copperplate 33BC, 50 point), and enter the text you want to work with in the new channel.

3 Choose black as the foreground color and white for the background color.

4 Make Channel #1 active. You should still be able to see the active selection. If you don't, then load the selection Channel #2 to make the area inside the type active.

5 Now, choose Select➡Feather and set the amount to 4 pixels. You may find that varying this number produces a better effect—it depends on the typeface you choose. Choose Edit➡Fill (Foreground Color, Opacity: 100%, Normal). Choose Select➡None (Command-D) [Control-D].

6 Apply Filter➡Stylize➡Emboss (Angle: 135°, Height: 6, Amount: 100%) to raise the text. The angle setting determines the direction of the primary source of light.

7 Load the selection Channel #2 (Invert selection). Click the foreground color and change it to 50% gray by changing the B setting of the HSB to 50%.

8 Choose Edit➡Fill (Foreground Color, Opacity: 100%, Normal). Choose Select➡None (or Command-D) [Control-D].

9 This is the magical step. Go to Image➡Adjust➡Curves (Command-M) [Control-M]. Click the Load button and find the MagicCurve file, or re-create the curve you see here. The more precise it is, the better it works. Click OK.

Do you see this?

10 Load the selection Channel #2. Then choose Image➡Adjust➡Invert (Command-I) [Control-I].

11 Choose Select➡Modify➡Expand (1 pixel). Choose Select➡Inverse. Choose white as the foreground color (press X) and press (Option-Delete) [Alt-Delete] to make the background white.

Expand Selection

Expand By: **1** pixels

OK

Cancel

Untitled-1 @ 50% (#1)

ØREØS

50%   Doc: 220K/96K

Levels

Channel: #1

Input Levels: 0   1.00   255

Output Levels: 0   240

OK

Cancel

Load...

Save...

Auto

☐ Preview

---

12 Go to Select➡Inverse, then Image➡Adjust➡Levels (Command-L) [Control-L]. In this dialog box, change the Output Levels white point (the lower-right box) from 255 to 240 and click OK.

TIP You can use the Input Levels in the Levels dialog box to fine-tune the greys in the chrome. Moving the middle (gray) slider to the left will brighten things up.

13 Add a background and experiment with adding a bit of color to your type.

Untitled-1 @ 50% (#1)

ØREØS

50%   Doc: 220K/96K

50

Chrome 2

Follow the steps for creating Plastic type (page 174) with the following exceptions:

4 Do not deselect the selection.

5 Return to the composite channel.

6 Deselect the text (Command-D) after this step.

7 Skip this step.

Now, choose Filter➡Stylize➡ Find Edges. You may prefer using Find Edges & Invert. Choose Edit➡ Select All, then copy (Command-C) [Control-C] the image. Go to the RGB channel (Command-0) [Control-0], and paste the text into this composite channel. That's it.

VARIATIONS

Adding a little color to the chrome might be the final touch it needs. You need to convert the file to a color mode first. I chose CMYK (choose Mode➡CMYK). Choose Image➡Adjust➡Curves (Command-M) [Control-M]. Best results come from working in the color channels one at a time. In these two variations, I bent the Cyan curve up a little, then down a little. You may find it easier to use the Hue/Saturation (Command-U) [Control-U] dialog box, in which you can slide the Hue slider to the left and right to produce subtle color changes.

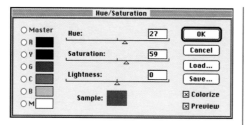

Adding a lot of color can change your chrome to something that looks more like gold. Choose Image➡Adjust➡Hue/Saturation (Command-U) [Control-U]. Make sure the preview box is checked so you can see what you're doing. Click the Colorize checkbox in the lower right, and try these values: Hue: 27, Saturation: 59, Lightness: 0. ■

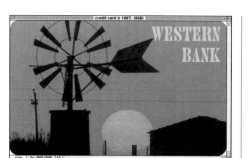

1 Open the picture you want to use as your credit card background or create a new file. This stock photo comes from Digital Stock.

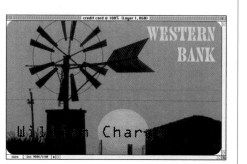

2 Use the Type tool to enter the text and move it to where you want it to fall on the image. We used the OCR-A font at 30 points to achieve a more realistic look. Change this layer name to "Text" and leave all other settings at their default.

3 Choose Duplicate Layer from the Layer palette menu and name it "Shadow." You should now have a total of three layers in your file.

4 Make the Text layer the active layer. For ease, you might also want to make it the only visible layer, too. Make sure Preserve Transparency is not checked, and apply Filter➡Blur➡Gaussian Blur. A setting of 2 pixels was used for this image. If your type is considerably larger, use a higher pixel setting.

5 Apply Filter➡Stylize➡Find Edges to the text layer. This is the beginning of the raised effect.

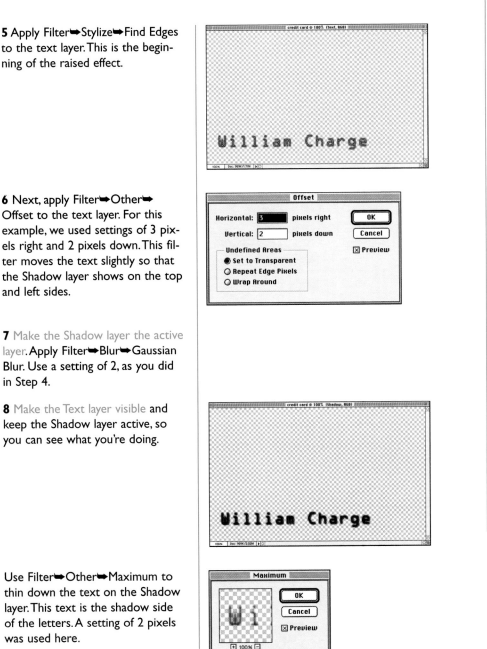

6 Next, apply Filter➡Other➡ Offset to the text layer. For this example, we used settings of 3 pixels right and 2 pixels down. This filter moves the text slightly so that the Shadow layer shows on the top and left sides.

7 Make the Shadow layer the active layer. Apply Filter➡Blur➡Gaussian Blur. Use a setting of 2, as you did in Step 4.

8 Make the Text layer visible and keep the Shadow layer active, so you can see what you're doing.

Use Filter➡Other➡Maximum to thin down the text on the Shadow layer. This text is the shadow side of the letters. A setting of 2 pixels was used here.

55

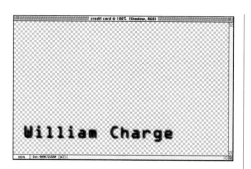

9 Make all three layers visible. Move the Shadow layer to make it the layer directly below the Text layer. This puts the Shadow layer behind the Text layer so it doesn't obscure the words.

10 Make the Text layer active. Adjust the Opacity level to 70%. This lets the background image show through and reduces the harshness of the shadows.

If you like the way the image shows through the text, you can flatten the image and stop now. But if you want the look of ink printed onto the "raised" letters, keep going.

11 To add the ink, make the Shadow layer active and duplicate it by choosing Duplicate Layer from the Layers palette menu. Name the layer "Ink." Move the Ink layer above the other layers in the Layers palette.

Use Filter➡Other➡Offset to move this layer the same amount that you moved the Text layer in Step 6. The Offset dialog box has the same settings you used the last time the effect was applied, so all you need to do is click OK.

Use Filter➡Other➡Maximum with a setting of 1 pixel to thin the text even more. At higher settings, the letters may start to fill in, so do some experimenting first!

12 Choose Image➡Adjust➡Invert (Command-I)[Control-I] to make the text white.

VARIATION

To colorize the type, choose Image➡Adjust➡Hue/Saturation. Be sure to check the Colorize check-box first to give you the appropriate sliders to work with. Adjust the sliders until you get the color you want. You can also try different backgrounds before you flatten your image. When you're done, flatten the image and charge it! ■

57

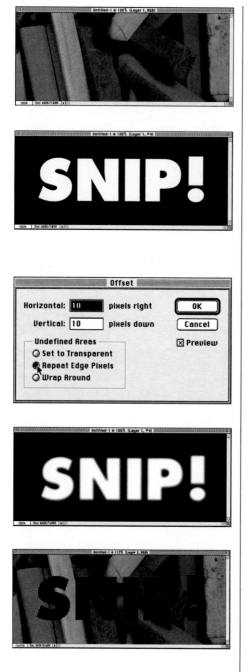

1 Open a new file or a file with an image you want to cut the text from.

2 Create a new channel (Channel #4). Choose white as the foreground color and use the Type tool to enter the text. While the text selection is still active, save the selection (Channel #5).

Deselect the text (Command-D) [Control-D].

3 Now, apply Filter➡Blur➡ Gaussian Blur (3.5 pixels). Then choose Filter➡Other ➡Offset (10 pixels right, 10 pixels down, and make sure to choose the Repeat Edge Pixels option). This channel is the shadow that appears behind the text.

4 Return to the composite channel (Command-~) [Control-~], and create a new layer (Layer 1).

5 Load the selection you saved in Step 2 (Channel #5) and fill it with black, or any other color you want to use for the shadow.

6 Keep the selection active. Now, choose Select➡Load Selection, activate the shadow channel (#4), and choose the Intersect with Selection option.

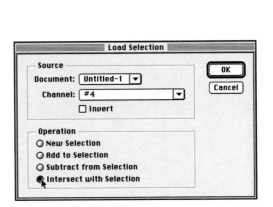

The active selection should look like this.

7 Change the foreground color to the color you want to make the background. Press (Option-Delete) [Alt-Delete] to fill the selection, deselect it (Command-D) [Control-D] and you're done. No cuts, no bleeding, no errors.

TIP **If you want to fine tune the shadow (brighten, soften, change its color), then load the selection Channel #5. Now load the selection Channel #4, selecting the Subtract from Selection option. The shadow is now selected.**

59

VARIATIONS

If you want to cut through one image to see another underneath, before opening the file containing the foreground image in Step 1, open the file containing the background image. Copy the part of the image you want to use as the background. Complete all the steps above except Step 7. Instead choose Edit➡Paste Into. Presto! If you need to move the background image, drag it around using the Move tool—but only if you didn't deselect it first.

In Step 1 create a new file with a white image area and do the entire exercise. In Step 7, choose white as the foreground color. The type needs a soft outline to separate the foreground from the white background, so load the selection #5 you saved in Step 2, and choose Edit➡Stroke (1 pixel, Center, 10% Opacity, Normal).

You can apply this technique to anything you put in a channel. Try using a hard-edged paintbrush and adding text or art into the channel, like the steam curls in this image. ■

1 Open the QuakeStripes preset file included on the CD-ROM, choose Select➡All and copy the image to the clipboard (Command-C) [Control-C]. Close the file (Command-W) [Control-W].

2 Create a new file. (Be sure to select RGB mode.) Create a new channel (Channel #4). Paste the clipboard into this new channel (Command-V) [Control-V]. Use Layer➡Transform➡Scale to fill the channel with the stripes if it does not fit properly.

TIP The width of the stripes in this file may not be a good width for the text size you want to distort. If the stripes are too small, then use the Scale command to make them larger. If they are too big, then scale them down, copy them, paste the copy back into the channel, and move the copy so it continues the striped pattern. Repeat if necessary.

62

TOOLBOX

QuakeStripes preset file

3 Return to the composite channel (Command-~) [Control-~]. Change the foreground color to a color for the text. Use the Type tool to enter the text. We used Helvetica Bold Oblique at 65 points for this example. If you do not choose an oblique font, then check the Italic style option. It is also important to give the letters some room to move. We increased the spacing to 10.

4 Load the transparency selection for the new layer containing the type (Layer 2), and save the selection (Channel #5). Flatten the image before you continue.

5 Move the letters in pieces by using the two channels to select only certain parts of the letters. To select the first part, choose Select➧Load Selection and choose Channel #4 with the Subtract from Selection option checked.

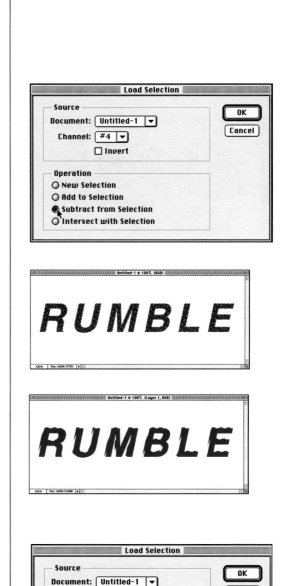

6 Press (Command-J) [Control-J] to create a new layer via copy. Make sure the Move tool is active (press V). Now use the arrow keys to move the text to the left and upward. We pressed the up arrow key 3 times and the left arrow key 5 times. Deselect the text (Command-D) [Control-D].

7 Make the Background layer active. Load the text selection (Channel #5), then load the stripes selection (Channel #4) with the Intersect with Selection option checked.

63

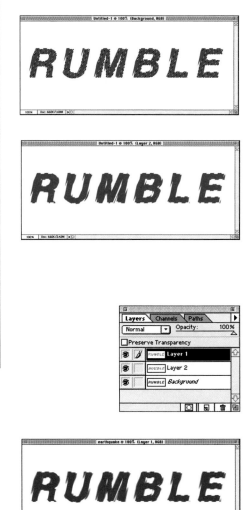

8 Press (Command-J) [Control-J] to create a new layer via copy. Make sure the Move tool is active (press V). Again, use the arrow keys to move the text. This time move the selection to the right and down. We pressed the down arrow key 3 time and the right arrow key 5 times. Deselect the text (Command-D) [Control-D].

9 You can stop at Step 8 but if you want to add some more realism, try adding some motion blurs. First, note that Photoshop 4 has created some new layers in the process of creating this image. Activate each of those layers and apply Filter➡ Blur➡Motion Blur (we used a setting of 5). Remember, don't be afraid to experiment!

VARIATIONS

Two extra steps make this variation. Before Step 5, and after loading the text selection in Step 7,
choose Select➡Modify➡Border
(7 pixels).

Add color. After copying the text
selection onto a new layer in Steps
6 and 8, change the foreground
color and press (Option-Delete)
[Alt-Delete] to fill the slices with
the new color. ■

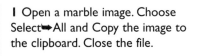

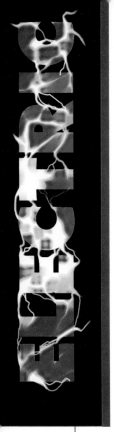

1 Open a marble image. Choose Select➡All and Copy the image to the clipboard. Close the file.

2 Create a new file for your final image, choosing white for the Background color in the New File dialog. Create a new channel (#4), and paste in the marble image from the clipboard. Move it around so a fair amount of white streaks are in view.

3 Apply Filter➡Blur➡Gaussian Blur (10 pixels).

4 Apply Filter➡Other➡Minimum (10 pixels). This step creates the bright bolts.

TOOLBOX

Alien Skin's Glow filter

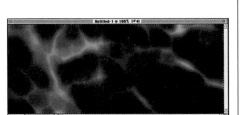

You should now have something similar to this.

5 Apply Filter➟Sharpen➟Unsharp Mask (344%, 9.1 pixels, 9 levels).

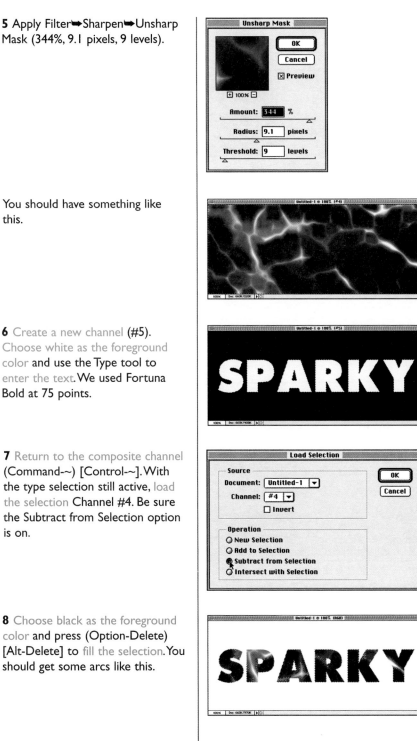

You should have something like this.

6 Create a new channel (#5). Choose white as the foreground color and use the Type tool to enter the text. We used Fortuna Bold at 75 points.

7 Return to the composite channel (Command-~) [Control-~]. With the type selection still active, load the selection Channel #4. Be sure the Subtract from Selection option is on.

8 Choose black as the foreground color and press (Option-Delete) [Alt-Delete] to fill the selection. You should get some arcs like this.

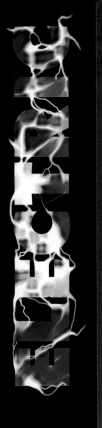

9 With the selection still active, choose Image➡Adjust➡Color Balance. We used the following settings for this example (Midtones: +70,–100,+3 Highlights: +100, –8, –60) to get a red set of bolts. Use (Midtones: –80,–100,+90, Highlights: –85, 0, +50) for blue bolts. You can experiment here to find different color choices. Also, this effect looks best if you are creating RGB artwork because it can retain more vibrant colors than in CMYK mode.

10 Load the type selection (Channel #5) and choose Select➡ Inverse. Press (Option-Delete) [Alt-Delete] to fill in the background with black. Deselect the selection (Command-D) [Control-D].

11 Now use the Smudge tool with a fairly small brush size to extend some of the electric bolts.

12 When you are satisfied, switch to the Airbrush tool. Choose an appropriate brush size and click in a region you are about to airbrush while temporarily holding down the (Option) [Alt] key (to switch to the Eyedropper tool). This chooses a foreground color that is close to the area you are about to paint. Then carefully airbrush in some bolts.

Vary the airbrush size to get some more realistic effects.

13 Choose Image➡Adjust➡ Brightness/Contrast (Contrast: 25).

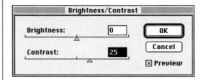

VARIATION

After you are finished, try adding a glow and some text. This glow was added very quickly using Alien Skin's Glow filter. ■

There are a number of ways to raise text in Photoshop. The first method shown here is a shortcut to embossing type. The Lighting Effects filter relieves you from having to find the highlights and shadows. The second method is the traditional (Can you use that word when you're talking about Photoshop?) method that uses separate channels for the highlights and shadows, enabling you to edit and re-edit those areas of the type.

Embossed 1

1 Create a new RGB file or open a file containing the surface you want to emboss. Whichever you choose, the file must be in RGB mode because the Lighting Effects filter only works in RGB mode.

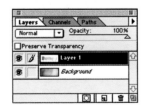

2 Create a new channel, and use the Type Mask tool to enter the text. We used Myriad Bold at 100 points. Fill the text with white. Keep the selection active, and choose Filter➡Blur➡Gaussian Blur (4 pixels) to blur only the inside of the type. The lower the pixel radius you use when blurring, the softer and slighter the edges of the text will be. Make the Background layer active. Now choose Layer➡New➡ Layer Via Copy (Command-J) [Control-J]]. This creates the text on a separate layer.

TOOLBOX

Alien Skin's Inner Bevel

EmbossLightStyles file

3 Choose Filter➡Render➡Lighting Effects. Either choose the Emboss-LightStyles preset from the pop-up menu or adjust the settings as you see them here. If it doesn't show up in the list, see page 242 to find out how to load it from the CD-ROM. Make sure that you position the light far enough away from the text that the letters aren't completely washed out. Click OK and you're finished.

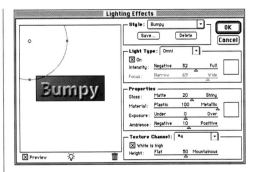

TIP **If you want the same lighting effects on your background, make that layer active and apply the same lighting effect settings. Another way to try this technique is to load the texture channel in the Lighting Effects filter with the type channel you created in Step 2 (Channel #4).**

Embossed 2

Created by Craig Swanson

I Create a new file or open a file containing the surface you want to emboss. We filled this background image with blue.

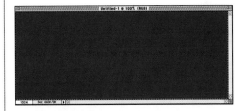

2 Create a new channel (Channel #4). Use the Type tool to enter the text you want to apply the effect to in the new channel. Again, we used Myriad Bold at 100 points. Deselect the text (Command-D) [Control-D].

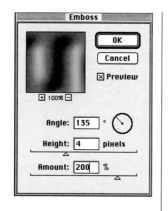

3 Duplicate Channel #4 to create Channel #5. To soften the edges, apply Filter➡Blur➡Gaussian Blur (8 pixels). Apply Filter➡Stylize➡ Emboss (135°, 4 pixels, 200%). The type should now look like this.

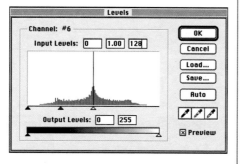

4 Duplicate Channel #5 to create Channel #6. To isolate the shadow areas in this channel, choose Image➡Adjust➡Levels (Input Levels: 0, 1, 128).

5 Load the selection **Channel #4.**
Check the Invert checkbox.
Choose white as the background
color and press Delete. Deselect
the background (Command-D)
[Control-D] and invert the image
(Image➡Adjust➡ Invert). This channel is used as the selection for the
shadows.

6 To make the channel for the
highlights, make Channel #5 active.
Choose Image➡Adjust➡Invert and
then Image➡Adjust➡Levels (Input
Levels: 0, 1, 128).

7 Load the selection Channel #4.
Check the Invert checkbox.
Choose white as the background
color and press Delete. Deselect
the background (Command-D)
[Control-D]. Choose Image➡
Adjust➡Invert. Now you have a
selection channel for the highlights.

8 Return to the composite channel
(Command-~) [Control-~], and
load the selection **Channel #6.**
Choose black as the foreground
color. Now press (Option-Delete)
[Alt-Delete] to fill in the shadows,
and then a second time if you want
a stronger edge.

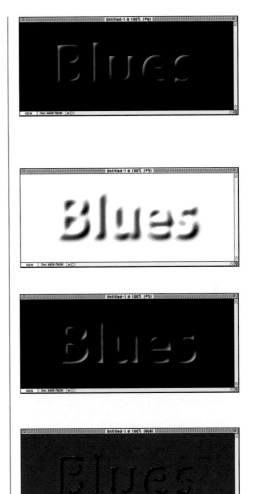

9 Finally, load the selection Channel #5 and choose white as the foreground color. Now press (Option-Delete) [Alt-Delete] to fill in the highlights. If you want a stronger edge, press (Option-Delete) [Alt-Delete] a second time.

TIP The advantage to Emboss 2 is that you can load the highlight and shadow selections again if you want to make alterations.

VARIATION

Another quick way to create embossed type is with the Inner Bevel filter—part of Alien Skin's Eye Candy (formerly called Black Box) collection of filters.

Create a new file. Use the Type tool to enter the text you want to apply the effect to in the new channel. Keep the selection active as you return to the composite channel (Command-~) [Control-~]. Apply Filter➡Alien Skin➡Inner Bevel 2.1. Experiment with the settings. Here's what we came up with after loading the selection again and raising the contrast inside the text. ■

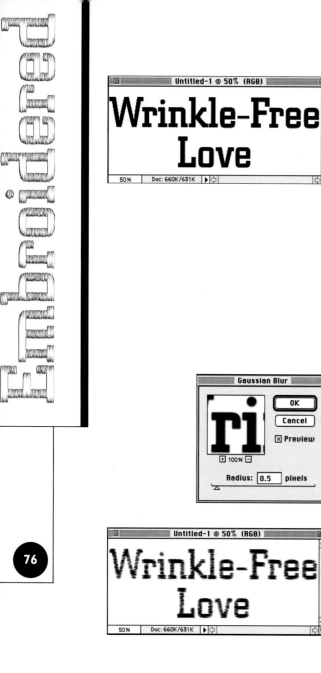

1 Create a new file. Set the foreground color to black (press D). Use the Type tool to enter the text. We used City Medium at 70 points for this example. Flatten the Image.

TIP The point size and thickness of the font are important in this technique because the Wind filter can really blow small or thin type away. If you want smaller type, we still suggest you use 70 points and choose Image➡Effects➡ Scale to reduce the type when you're finished.

2 Choose Filter➡Blur➡Gaussian Blur (0.5 pixels). The thicker the font, the higher the pixel radius should be.

3 Choose Filter➡Stylize➡Wind (Wind, Left). Press (Command-Option-F) [Control-Alt-F] to bring back the last filter dialog box, and switch the Wind direction to Right.

4 Choose Image➡Adjust➡Invert
(Command-I) [Control-I].

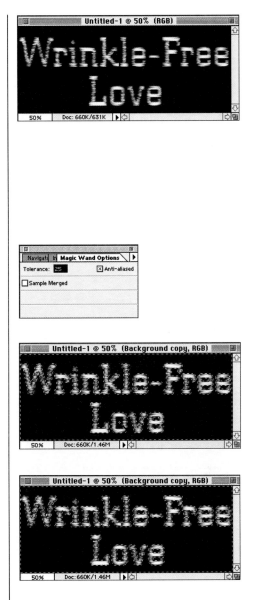

5 Choose Duplicate Layer from the
Layers palette menu to create the
Background copy layer. Click OK to
accept the defaults.

6 Double-click the Magic Wand
tool. Find the Magic Wand Tool
Options palette (it's hiding some-
where on your screen) and change
the Tolerance setting to 25. With
the Magic Wand, click in the black
area of the image. You also need to
select the enclosed areas within letters such as "e" and "o" by holding
the Shift key and clicking within
these areas. Press Delete.

7 Deselect the text (Command-D) [Control-D], and choose Filter➡ Stylize➡Emboss (135°, 5 pixels, 100%).

8 In the Layers palette click the Blending Modes pop-up menu and choose Lighten. Leave the opacity at 100%.

9 Flatten the image.

TIP To copy the type onto another background, use the Magic Wand tool again to select the black area around the type and in the middle of letters (as in Step 6). Choose Select➡ Inverse, then copy the type (Command-C) [Control-C]. Go to the file you want to paste the text into, and paste it in (Command-V) [Control-V].

VARIATIONS

Add subtle color to the thread. Use the Magic Wand tool to select the area around the type (as in Step 6). Choose Select➡Inverse. Then choose Image➡Adjust➡ Hue/ Saturation, and click the Colorize checkbox. Use the Hue slider to find the color you're looking for, and drop the Saturation slider to control the brightness of the color. For this variation we set the Saturation at 20.

Change the color of the thread. Before entering the text in Step 1, fill the background with a dark version of a color near the complement of the thread color you want to use (for example, a dark blue if you are using orange thread). Don't use black for the foreground color. Instead, choose as the foreground color a light version of the color of the thread you want. Complete the rest of the steps and you're finished. ■

79

TOOLBOX

Natural Gas
Palette

Created by Sal Gilberto
Revision by David Lai

1 Create a new file. Choose Image➡Mode➡Grayscale and press D to set the foreground color to black. Press (Option-Delete) [Alt-Delete] to fill the image with black.

2 Choose white as the foreground color (press X) and use the Type tool to enter the text. For best results, use a large sans serif font (in this example, we used Micro-Technic at 65 points). Set the text toward the bottom of the window so there is enough room for the flames.

3 Choose Select➡Load Selection (Layer 1 Transparency), and with the text selection still active, save the current selection (Channel #2). Switch to the Layers palette and flatten the image.

4 Deselect the text (Command-D) [Control-D], and rotate the image 90 degrees counterclockwise (Image➡Rotate Canvas➡90° CCW).

5 Apply Filter➡Stylize➡Wind
(Blast, Left). The larger your text,
the more wind it needs. If you are
using a smaller point size, Wind
might do the job. Larger text might
need the Blast applied twice. You
should see something like this.

6 Return the image to its original
orientation by rotating it 90
degrees clockwise (Image➡Rotate
Canvas➡90° CW).

7 Apply Filter➡Stylize➡Diffuse
(Normal).

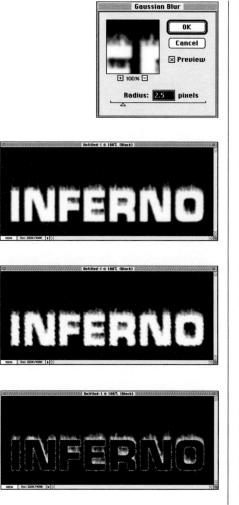

8 Apply Filter→Blur→Gaussian Blur (Radius: 2.5).

The image should now look like this.

9 Apply Filter→Distort→Ripple. Use the default settings (100, Medium).

10 Load the selection Channel #2. Choose Select→Modify→Contract (2 pixels) and Select→Feather (1 pixel). Choose black as the foreground color (press D) and press (Option-Delete) [Alt-Delete] to fill the selection. Deselect the selection. (Command-D) [Control-D].

TIP If you want a lighter, more realistic-looking flame, adjust the gray values before converting the image to color. Choose Image→Adjust→Levels (Command-L). Try these settings for the Input Levels values: 0, 3.46, 190.

11 Convert the image to Indexed Color mode (Image➥Mode➥ Indexed Color). Choose Image➥ Mode➥Color Table and choose Black Body from the pop-up menu.

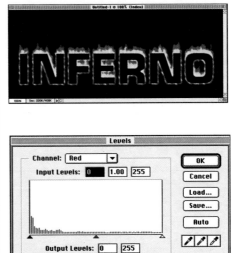

After changing color tables, your type should look like it's on fire.

TIP You can use the Levels dialog box to adjust the color and height of the flames. Choose Image➥ Adjust➥ Levels (Command-L) [Control-L]. It helps to work in the Red and Green channels separately.

83

For this variation, we used black text on a white background. Use all the same steps except skip Step 10.

After Step 10, adjust the Output Levels (Command-L) [Control-L] white point to 240. In Step 11, use the Natural Gas palette (included on the CD-ROM accompanying this book) instead of the Black Body palette, then convert the image to RGB and apply Filter➡Blur➡Blur.

Now don't light any matches.

Create a flaming shadow by choosing Image➡Adjust➡Invert ((Command-I) [Control-I]) right before doing Step 11.

In a grayscale file, create a new channel (#2) and enter the text in that channel. Make the Black channel active. Load the selection Channel #2. Fill it with black. Deselect the text. Apply the Gaussian Blur filter (5 pixels). Load the selection Channel #2. Fill it with black. Choose Filter➡ Render➡Difference Clouds. Deselect the text, and choose Filter➡Render➡Difference Clouds. Do Step 11. ▪

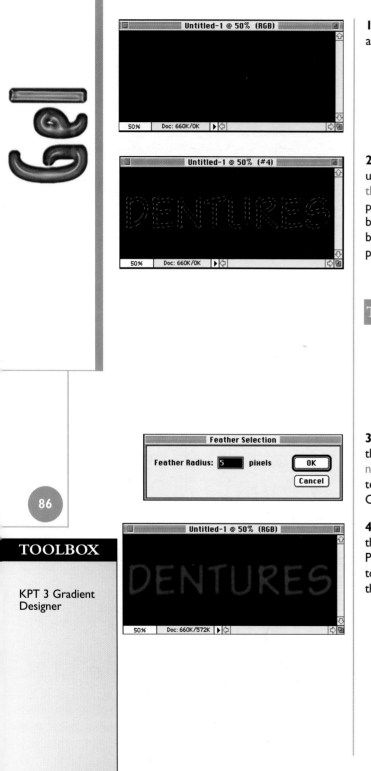

1 Create a new file. Fill the image area with black.

2 Create a new channel (#4) and use the Type Mask tool to enter the text. We used Tekton Bold at 75 points. This technique works with both simple and complicated fonts, but keep in mind that you have to play with the settings to get it right.

TIP If the font you choose has hard edges, choose Select➡ Modify➡Smooth (5 pixels). If that doesn't round your selection enough, then smooth it again until it has a good round contour.

3 Fill the type selection with white, then return to the composite channel (Command-~) [Control-~]. The text selection should still be active. Choose Select➡Feather (5 pixels).

4 Choose a foreground color for the gel. We used 100% Magenta. Press (Option-Delete) [Alt-Delete] to fill the text selection. Deselect the text (Command-D) [Control-D].

86

TOOLBOX

KPT 3 Gradient
Designer

5 To add a gloss to the text, use the Plastic Wrap filter. This filter produces very different results depending upon the size of the area selected. Therefore, apply the filter to each letter one at a time. First, load the text selection Channel #4.

6 Choose the Lasso tool, and hold down the (Option) [Alt] and Shift key while you draw around the letter you want to select. The selection you draw can be as sloppy as you want as long as you don't run over any of the other selection lines. After you complete the loop around the letter and let go of the mouse button, only that letter is selected.

7 Now, choose Filter➡Artistic➡ Plastic Wrap. Use these settings: Highlight Strength: 15, Detail: 9, Smoothness: 7. Use the preview to test the best settings for your text and to find something that looks like this figure. You may need to use different settings for each letter to get the best results.

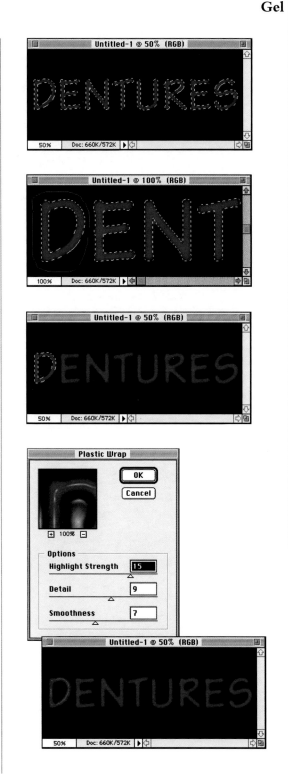

87

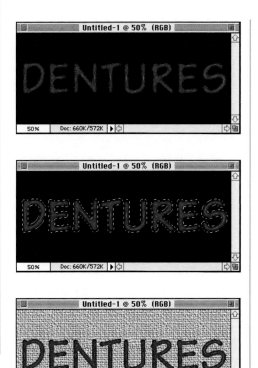

8 For each letter, load the text selection Channel #4, then repeat Step 6. After each new letter is selected, press (Command-F) [Control-F] to apply the Plastic Wrap filter with the same settings.

9 To make a selection for the text, load the text selection Channel #4. Then choose Select➡Modify➡ Expand. Start with an expansion of 1 pixel. You want to expand the selection so that it includes almost all of the blurred color.

10 With this selection, you can copy the text and paste onto any background you want. We applied a 2 pixel stroke around the text to give it more definition.

VARIATIONS

Outlines

If you want to create an outline gel text, you can insert these steps after Step 2 to change the solid text to outlines. It is difficult to get this technique to work if you choose a narrow or complicated font, so keep it simple and let the effect carry your message.

Choose Select➡Modify➡ Contract (8 pixels). We used 8 pixels, but use whatever works for your text to create an outline like the one shown in this figure. Fill the selection with black. Then simply complete the rest of the steps.

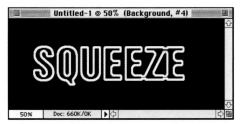

Or try this: After finishing the steps above, copy your image and do whatever you want to it. In this example, we copied the text to a yellow background, smudged the edges of the text, and applied Filter➡Sharpen➡Unsharp Mask (55%, 3 pixels, 0 levels). Smudging the text helps incorporate the edges with the background.

KPT 3 Gradient Designer

We used the Shelley Andante font for this variation. After completing the steps, we created a new layer, loaded the text selection Channel #4 into the new layer, and filled it with white. With the selection still active, we applied Filter➡KPT 3.0➡KPT Gradient Designer 3.0. We used the Tacky Wacky preset, then customized it. Finally, I chose Color from the Layers palette menu. ▪

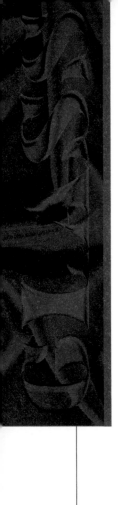

GlassLightingStyles
file

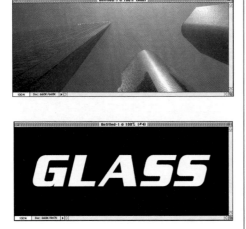

This effect turns your dull, boring text into a shiny piece of see-through type. The smudging in Steps 7 through 12 makes it look ultra-realistic.

1 Open the image you want to use as a background. We used this photo from Digital Stock for this example.

2 Create a new channel (Channel #4) and use the Type tool enter your text into it. We used Serpentine Bold Oblique at 80 points for this example. Select➡None (Command-D) [Control-D] so you have no active selection.

3 Duplicate Channel #4 and rename it Blur #1 (to make remembering what the channel is easier). To the Blur #1 channel, apply Filter➡Blur➡Gaussian Blur with a setting of 3 pixels.

4 Duplicate Channel Blur #1 and rename it Blur #2. Apply Filter➡ Other➡Offset with a setting of −4 pixels right and −3 pixels down.

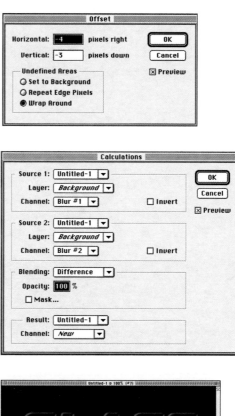

5 Now apply Image➡Calculations. Both Source options and the Result option should be set to the name of your current document (they probably are, by default). In Source 1, set Layer: Background and Channel: Blur #1. For Source 2, set Layer: Background, Channel: Blur #2. Set the Blending mode to Difference and the Opacity to 100%. Leave the Invert and Mask boxes unchecked.

You should get something like this.

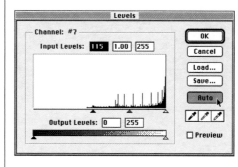

6 Choose Image➡Adjust➡Invert to invert the new channel (Channel #7), and apply Image➡Adjust➡ Levels (Command-L) [Control-L]. Click the Auto button to adjust the levels automatically.

The result should be an image with more contrast.

7 Now return to the composite channel (Command-~) [Control-~] and get ready for some fun! Load the selection Channel #4 (the channel with the original, unblurred text). Choose Make Work Path from the Paths palette menu.

8 Choose the Smudge tool and choose a large soft-edged brush from the Brushes palette. In the Smudge Tool Options palette, set the pressure of the Smudge tool to 23%.

9 Load the selection Channel #4 again. Onscreen you'll see the path and the selection active. If not, bring the Paths palette to the front, click the path in the palette, then choose Make Selection.

10 Choose Stroke Path from the Paths palette menu, and make sure the Smudge tool is active in the Tool palette. After a few moments, the image inside the selection will be smudged somewhat. Because the selection from Channel #4 was loaded, the blurring only took place inside the selection, not outside.

11 Because glass distorts images more at the outer edges, a little more smudging needs to be done, but closer to the edges. With both the path and Channel #4 still active and the Smudge tool selected, choose a medium-sized feathered brush. Bump the pressure up to 40%.

12 Once again, stroke the path (choose Stroke Path from the Paths palette) with the Smudge tool.

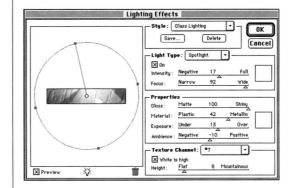

13 You're finished with the path, so it can be turned off. Simply shift-click its name in the Paths palette. Keep Channel #4 an active selection, however.

14 Now comes the fun part— making it shiny. Bring up the Filter➡Render➡Lighting Effects dialog box. If you loaded the GlassLightingStyles file from the CD ROM, choose it from the pre-set pop-up menu. If it's not there, just look at the figure to get the settings. Also, be sure that the Texture Channel option is set to Channel #7 (or whatever channel was created when the two blurred channels were combined).

93

15 If the preset settings don't give you the ideal result, then tweak any of the settings in the Light Type or Properties sections of the dialog box. Try playing with the light direction and size, too. You can also adjust the Height slider to make the text appear bumpier or flatter. Don't, however, change the Texture Channel setting. It should be set to the channel that resulted when the two blurred channels were combined. This channel is used to determine where the highlights and shadows occur on the text. If you change it to a different channel, your text probably appears really flat with very few highlights, if any! After clicking OK, you should get some nice, bright text.

16 To add an extra gloss to the text, make sure that Channel #4 (the regular text channel) is still loaded. Apply Filter➡Sharpen➡Unsharp Mask with the settings Amount: 61%, Radius: 2.3 pixels, and Threshold: 0 levels.

94

This sharpens the image inside the text and nudges the contrast up a smidgen. Be sure to note how the smudging done earlier really adds to the believability factor! ■

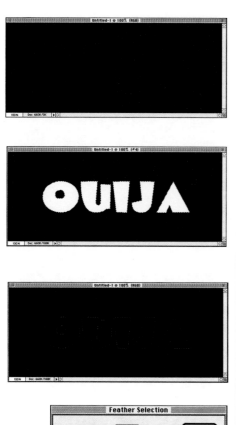

1 Create a new file. Choose black as the background color. Select➡ All and press Delete to fill the image with black. Select➡None (Command-D) [Control-D].

2 Create a new channel (Channel #4). Choose white as the foreground color. With the Type tool, enter the text you want to apply the effect to in the new channel. We used FontHead Design's BlueMoon at 80 points for this example.

3 Return to the composite channel. (Command-~) [Control-~]. Your text should still be the active selection. If it's not, then load the selection Channel #4.

Feather Selection

Feather Radius: 10 pixels OK Cancel

4 Choose Select➡Feather and use a setting of 10 pixels. Don't worry if it looks like part of your letters disappear, particularly the skinny lines. They're still there, but the feathering decreased their strength, so Photoshop doesn't show them inside the area of active selection.

TOOLBOX

KPT 3 Gradient Designer

Alien Skin's Glow filter

5 Choose a glow color for the foreground color. We used bright green. Press (Option-Delete) [Alt-Delete] to fill the selection with the foreground color. You should get something like this.

6 Once again, choose Select➡ Feather and use a setting of 10 pixels. This feathers the already feathered selection, creating a really diffused look. Press (Option-Delete) [Alt-Delete] to fill the selection.

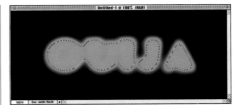

TIP If you try combining the two feathering steps by using a setting of 20 pixels for one feathering, the result will be a much less vibrant glow. By using two separate steps, you achieve a more neon-like effect.

7 Now load the selection Channel #4.

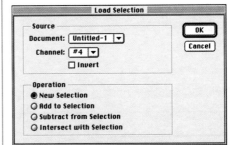

8 Choose black as the foreground color and press (Option-Delete) [Alt-Delete] to fill the selection. Select➡None (Command-D) [Control-D].

97

VARIATIONS

Blinding Glow

1 Follow Steps 1 through 7 listed previously. Choose Select➡Feather, and feather the selection just a little—3 pixels.

2 Choose white as the foreground color. Press (Option-Delete) [Alt-Delete] to fill the selection with white. Wow!

Filled Glow

1 Follow Steps 1 through 7 listed previously.

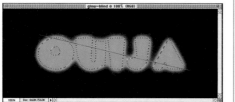

2 Choose white as the foreground color and black for the background color. Use the Gradient Fill tool (choose Foreground to Background from the Gradient pop-up menu in the Gradient Tool Options palette) and drag from the upper-left corner of the word to the lower-right corner.

3 Select➡None (Command-D) [Control-D]. You should end up with something like this.

Filled Glow with KPT 3 Gradient Designer

This variation is another way you can fill your type. Follow all the same steps for the Filled Glow above, except change Step 2 to:

2 Choose Filter➡KPT 3.0➡KPT Gradient Designer 3.0. Choose Blue Green Metal Cone from the submenu and set the mode to Linear Blend. Set the repeat option to Triangle A➡B➡A and click OK. (You can use any KPT setting you want.)

And here's what you get.

Ghosting

By using a second layer for the text, you can put type with a ghosted effect over an existing photo.

1 Create a new file with the image you want to use for the background. Create a new layer. Keep both layers visible, so you can see what you're doing, but make sure that Layer 1 is the active layer!

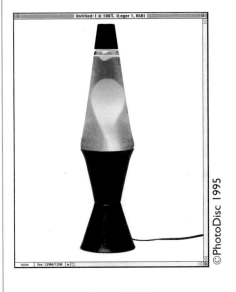

99

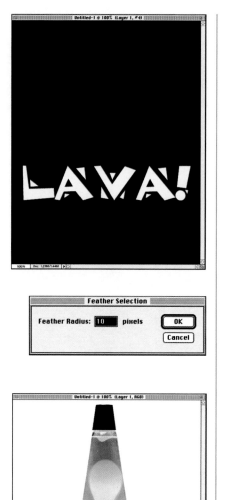

2 Create a new channel (Channel #4) and enter in your text with the Type tool. We used FontHead Design's Bonkers at 80 points here. Select➡None (Command-D) [Control-D].

3 Return to the composite channel and make Layer 1 the active layer. Load the selection Channel #4. Choose Select➡Feather and use a radius of 10 pixels.

4 Choose for the foreground color the color you want to use for the blur. We used a bright red. Press (Option-Delete) [Alt-Delete] to fill the selection with the foreground color. Press (Option-Delete) [Alt-Delete] again to intensify the color. Select➡None (Command-D) [Control-D].

5 If you want to remove color from the selection, then load the selection Channel #4 and choose Edit➡Clear.

Aura

1 Create a new file or create a new file with a white background.

2 Create a new channel and enter the text with the Type tool.

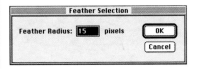

3 Return to the composite channel. Choose Select➡Feather using a setting of 15 pixels.

4 Choose a medium blue for the foreground color. Press (Option-Delete) [Alt-Delete] to fill the selection with the foreground color.

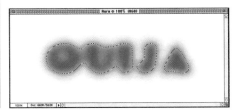

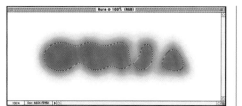

5 Again, choose Select➡Feather and use a setting of 15 pixels to diffuse the selection even more. Press (Option-Delete) [Alt-Delete] to fill the selection again.

6 Load the selection Channel #4. Choose black as the foreground color and fill the selection.

VARIATIONS

Alien Skin's Glow Filter

Here's another easy way to create a glow around your type.

1 Create a new file. We used a black background to make the glow stand out (press D, then (Option-Delete) [Alt-Delete]). Choose as the foreground color a color for the text. Enter the text with the Type Mask tool. Fill the text selection with the foreground color.

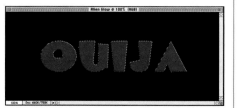

2 Choose as the foreground color a color for the glow. We used a light blue for a misty look.

3 Choose Filter➡Alien Skin➡ Glow. Set the Glow Color to Foreground. You can vary the settings for the Width (pixels) and the Opacity (%) of the glow. We used 40 pixels of Width and 80% Opacity. Set Opacity Dropoff to Thin. This makes the glow look thin and hazy. If you want a more intense glow, try the Fat option.

4 Click OK and presto—a super easy glow! ■

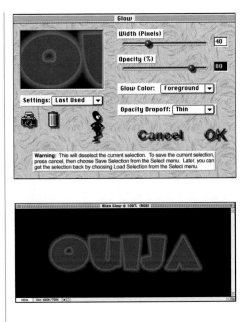

gradient

TRUE BLUE

TOOLBOX

KPT 3 Gradient
Designer

Filling text with a gradient is a very simple task, but it can produce great effects. As soon as you get to know your way around with masks, the possibilities will seem endless.

Setup

As always, the first steps: create a new file, then create a new channel (Channel #4), and use the Type tool to enter the text in the new channel (white text on a black background). After entering the text, return to the composite channel (Command-~) [Control-~].

> **TIP** To access the Gradient Tool Options palette, double-click the Gradient tool. Unless otherwise noted, we are assuming that the options are set to the defaults. You can revert to the defaults by choosing Reset Tool from the Gradient Tool Options palette menu.

Basic Gradient

Here's the basic gradient fill. The Gradient tool creates a blend between the foreground color and the background color. Choose the colors, then load the text selection (Channel #4). Now, use the Gradient tool, click where you want to start the gradient, and drag to the point where you want it to end. We also gave the text a white stroke to set it apart from the background (Edit➡Stroke (2 pixels, Outside, 100% Opacity, Normal Mode)).

Spectrum

The Gradient Tool Options palette offers some very useful variables. If you want a blend to include all of the colors that lie between the foreground color and the background color on the color spectrum, choose one of the spectrum options from the Style pop-up menu.

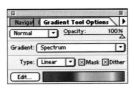

Transparency

Grading from a color to transparency is magic for your text. This option enables you to fade type into a background.

KPT 3 Gradient Designer

Use KPT 3 Gradient Designer for a more complex, but no more difficult, gradient. Sifting through the possibilities could consume hours, but don't forget to come back and read the rest of this section.

105

KPT 3 Procedural Blend

We used KPT 3 Gradient Designer for this one, too. We rendered the type using the Marquee method (page 124), then chose the Procedural Blend option in KPT 3 Gradient Designer. This option grades the color according to the values already in the type.

Graded Selections

Photographs and other images can be graded into a text selection. First copy an image from another file into the clipboard. Return to the empty file, load the text selection, then enter Quick Mask mode. Now use the Gradient tool as you did earlier, only choose Foreground to Transparent from the Gradient pop-up menu. The non-red areas in this window represent the areas where the photograph will be seen at full strength. Where there is solid red, the photograph will be completely masked or hidden. Areas in between will gradually fade the photograph. Press Q to exit the Quick Mask mode, and choose Edit➡Paste Into.

Blending Images

You can also use Quick Masks to blend two photographs together into a type selection.

Copy the first image from a separate file into the clipboard. Then, return to the file that contains your type, return to the composite channel (Command-~) [Control-~], and load the type selection. Press Q to enter Quick Mask mode. Use the Gradient tool, as described earlier (with Foreground to Transparent chosen from the Gradient pop-up menu), and drag from just above the bottom of the text to just below the top of the text. You should see something like this.

Exit Quick Mask mode (press Q), and choose Edit➡Paste Into to paste in the first image.

Now, copy the second image from a separate file into the clipboard. Again, return to the file that contains your type, return to the composite channel, and load the type selection. Press Q to enter Quick Mask mode. Use the Gradient tool and drag from just below the top of the text to just above the bottom of the text.

Exit Quick Mask mode (press Q), and choose Edit➡Paste Into to paste in the second image. That's it. We added a couple of strokes to the text selection to separate the text from the background.

Putting It All Together

This image combines several gradient techniques in a composite of several layered steps.

1 The background image is copied to the clipboard, then pasted into a graded mask.

2 A violet to transparent blend inside the type selection…

3 A cyan to transparent gradient inside the type selection…

4 A 2 pixel stroke is added to separate the type from the black background.

The final image. ■

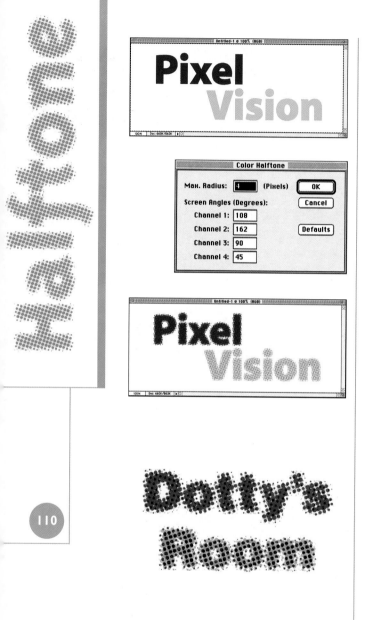

1 Create a new file. Enter the text with the Type tool that you want to use. We used Myriad Bold for this example. Here we used two different colors.

2 Choose Layer➡Flatten Image, then apply Filter➡Pixelate➡Color Halftone. Change the Max. Radius to 4 pixels and leave the Screen Angles at their defaults.

You should get something that looks like this.

VARIATIONS

For larger dots, change the Max. Radius in the Color Halftone dialog box. Here a setting of 8 pixels was used.

For something more abstract, go crazy with the Max. Radius! Try 20 pixels!

You can also create different effects by varying the Screen Angles in the Color Halftone dialog box. Here, all Screen angles were set to 0 (the Max. Radius was set to 6 pixels).

A bit of a wavy effect can be achieved by using Screen Angles of 0, 15, 30, 45. Again, Max. Radius was set to 6 pixels.

Keeping A Defined Edge

1 If you want to keep a solid edge on the text, create a new channel and enter the text with the Type tool.

2 Return to the composite channel, load the selection Channel #4 and fill with your choice of colors. Don't lose the selection yet!

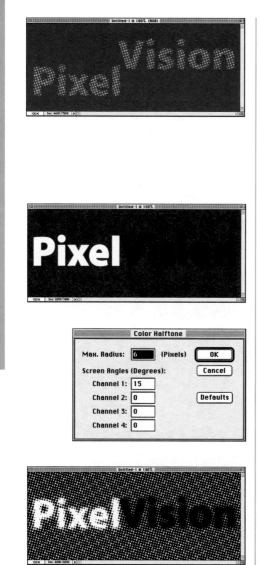

3 Choose Layer➡Flatten Image, then apply Filter➡Pixelate➡Color Halftone. We used 6 pixels for the Max. Radius and the default Screen Angles.

Black-and-White Halftone

You can also halftone black-and-white images.

1 Create a new grayscale file. Enter the text with the Type tool using different values of gray.

2 Choose Filter➡Pixelate➡Color Halftone. Use 6 pixels for the Max. Radius and 15 degrees for Channel 1's Screen Angle. Because this is a grayscale file, there is only one channel. The other values are ignored.

Your final image should look like this.

Color Halftone

Max. Radius:	6 (Pixels)	**OK**
Screen Angles (Degrees):		**Cancel**
Channel 1:	15	
Channel 2:	0	**Defaults**
Channel 3:	0	
Channel 4:	0	

Fun with Channels

1 Create a new image and choose a foreground color for the type (we used green). Then enter the text.

2 Use Image➡Duplicate twice to make two copies of the image in separate files.

3 With one of the duplicate images, convert to grayscale (Image➡ Mode➡Grayscale).

4 Next, use Image➡Mode➡Bitmap to convert the grayscale image to a bitmap. Photoshop will ask if you want to flatten the image's layer's— click OK. In the Bitmap dialog box, be sure the Output Resolution matches the Input Resolution. For Method, choose Halftone Screen.

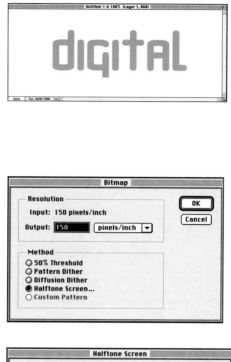

In the Halftone Screen dialog box, use a setting of 20 lines/inch for the Frequency, 30 degrees for the Angle, and Round for the Shape.

The image should now look something like this.

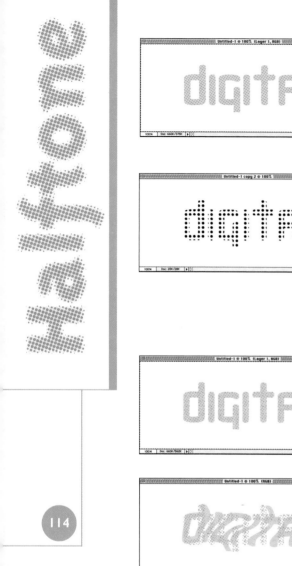

5 Select➡All and copy the image. Return to the original image and make the Red channel active. Paste the clipboard image into this channel, replacing what was already there. Return to the composite channel. You should have something like this.

6 Convert the other duplicate to grayscale. Then convert it to bitmap, but use the following settings. Frequency: 10 lines/inch, Angle: 0, Shape: Round. First, though, Photoshop will ask if you want to flatten the image's layer's— click OK. You should end up with something like what you see in this figure. Choose Select➡All to copy the image.

7 In the original image, paste the clipboard image into the Blue channel. Your final image should look like this.

8 For some added excitement, try distorting one of the channels. Here we used Filter➡Distort➡ Twirl with a setting of 56° on the Green channel.

Custom Patterns

You can also use a custom pattern for halftoning.

1 Before converting the mode to Bitmap, open a custom pattern. Keep in mind that smaller sizes tend to work better. Here we used the Deco pattern supplied in Photoshop. (Mac users will find it in Photoshop 4.0/Goodies/Brushes and Patterns/PostScript Patterns; Windows users should look in the Patterns directory inside the Photoshop directory.)

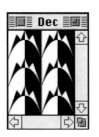

2 Select➡All and Edit➡Define Pattern to define the pattern.

3 Use Image➡Duplicate to make a copy of your original image. Then convert the mode of the duplicate to Grayscale (Image➡Mode➡Grayscale).

4 Choose Image➡Mode➡Bitmap and make sure both Input and Output numbers are the same. Choose Custom Pattern from the Method choices.

This uses your defined pattern for the dot size. The size of the pattern defines the frequency.

5 Copy the image and paste it into a channel in your original file. We pasted into the Green channel for this example. ■

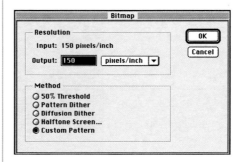

115

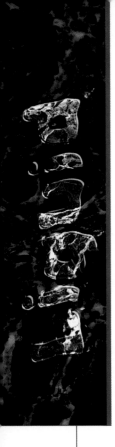

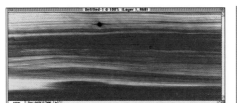

1 Create a new file (it must be an RGB file) or open an existing image. We used an image from D'Pix for this example. We changed the resolution to 150 dpi and cropped it down.

2 Create a new channel (#4), choose white as the foreground color, and use the Type tool to enter the text into Channel #4. This example uses Helvetica Condensed Black at 60 points. Choose Select➡None (Command-D) [Control-D].

3 You may be somewhat familiar with this step and the next few that follow it—they're very similar to the beginning steps of Melting text, just in a slightly different order. Use Image➡Rotate Canvas➡90° CW to rotate the image.

116

TOOLBOX

4 Apply Filter➡Stylize➡Wind with a setting of Wind and Left. Do this twice (press (Command-F) [Control-F]) to get a good amount of streakage.

You should have something like this.

5 You can now rotate the image back to right side up using Image➡Rotate Canvas➡90° CCW.

117

6 Apply Filter➡Brush Strokes➡ Spatter. Use settings of around 19 for the Radius and 15 for Smoothness. This adds some rough undulation to the text (don't worry—it'll be smoothed out in the next step).

Hey man, use
a coaster!

Stamp

OK
Cancel

100%

Options
Light/Dark Balance 34
Smoothness 11

7 To smooth out the edges, apply Filter➡Sketch➡Stamp with the setting at 34 for Light/Dark Balance and 11 for Smoothness.

Hey man, use
a coaster!

You should end up with something like this.

Wave

Number of Generators: 5

Type:
● Sine
○ Triangle
○ Square

OK
Cancel

Min. Max.
Wavelength: 42 170

Amplitude: 9 26

Horiz. Vert.
Scale: 28 % 21 %

Hey man, use
a coaster!

Undefined Areas:
○ Wrap Around
● Repeat Edge Pixels

Randomize

8 For more variation in the type, use Filter➡Distort➡Wave with the following settings: Generators: 5; Wavelength: 42, 170; Amplitude: 9, 26; Horiz.: 28; Vert.: 21; Type: Sine). Click the Randomize button a few times until the preview looks like what you're aiming for.

You should now have some nice, moderately wavy text.

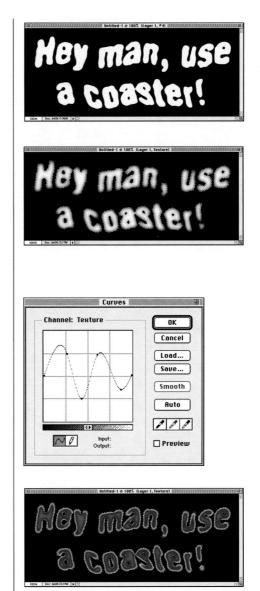

9 Duplicate Channel #4 and rename the new channel "Texture" because that's what it's going to be. In the Texture channel, load the selection Channel #4 and apply Filter➡Blur➡ Gaussian Blur (6 pixels). Because the selection is loaded, the blur only occurs on the inside of the text.

10 Bring up the Image➡Adjust➡ Curves dialog box, click the Load button, and find the LiquidCurve file.

119

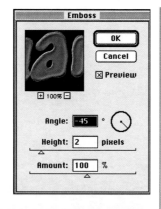

11 Still working in the Texture channel, but with the selection from Channel #4 still loaded, apply Filter➠Stylize➠Emboss. Use settings of Angle: −45°, Height: 2 pixels, and Amount: 100%. Your text should now look like it has a bit of a ridge around the outside of the letters.

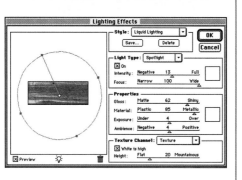

12 Select➠None (Command-D) [Control-D] and apply Filter➠ Blur➠ Gaussian Blur with a radius of 2 pixels to smooth out any jaggies.

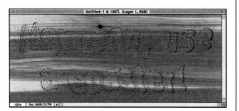

13 Now it's time to liquefy the text. Return to the composite channel and load the selection Channel #4 (the original text channel). Apply Filter➠Render➠ Lighting Effects and choose the LiquidLightStyles preset from the Style pop-up menu, with the Texture channel you created chosen in the Texture Channel pop-up menu. If you haven't installed it from the CD-ROM accompanying this book, simply copy these settings here.

This preset uses the Texture channel you created as, well, a texture. This results in highlights and shadows from the various levels of gray in the channel.

14 With Channel #4 still loaded, apply Filter➡Sharpen➡Unsharp Mask with a setting of Amount: 55%, Radius: 3.0 pixels, and Threshold: 0 levels. This brings up the contrast just a bit to give the illusion of looking through a liquid.

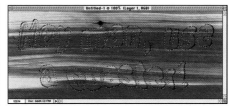

15 It may look good, but the high-lights still need to be added. In the Texture channel, load the selection Channel #4, and copy the channel (Command-C) [Control-C]. Return to the composite channel and create a new layer (Layer 1). Paste the copied image onto this layer and Select➡None (Command-D) [Control-D]. You should now have something like this.

16 To pull out some highlights, use Image➡Adjust-Brightness/Contrast with settings of Brightness: −13 and Contrast: +87.

17 Double-click Layer 1 (the one you just created) in the Layers palette. This brings up the Layer Options dialog box. Set the Mode to Luminosity and adjust the This Layer slider until the numbers read 130 and 235/255 (you can split the arrows by holding down the (Option) [Alt] key and moving just half of the slider triangle).

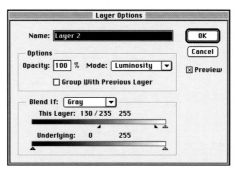

Adjusting this slider determines which values of gray are being used to increase the luminosity. By mov-ing the arrows around you can allow different grays to affect the underlying image.

121

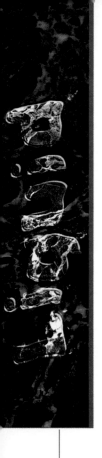

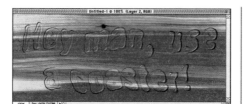

18 Finally, take down the opacity of Layer 1 to around 80%. This softens the intensity of the highlights a bit.

VARIATIONS

If you're looking for something other than clear liquid, try changing the light color in the Light Type section of the Lighting Styles dialog box in Step 13. Here, a medium green colored light was used. To change the light color, click the colored box at the right side of the Lighting Styles dialog box and choose a new color from the Color Picker.

If you're looking for an opaque sub-
stance, move the Materials slider in
the Lighting Effect dialog box from
Metallic all the way down to Plastic
when you render the text. When
you get to Step 16, where you
adjust the Brightness and Contrast
of Layer 1, use values of 100 for
Brightness and 25 for Contrast. For
Step 17, change the mode of Layer
1 to Luminosity, but skip the rest of
that step. For Step 18, adjust the
opacity of Layer 1 until the background is just barely visible. We
used 76% for this variation. ■

It doesn't get any easier than this. The Lighting Effects filter that comes with Photoshop (combined with the PlasticLightStyles preset file supplied on the *Type Magic* CD-ROM) does almost all the work for you.

1 Create a new file. Change the foreground and background colors to their default settings (press D). Create a new channel (#4). Use the Type tool to enter the text. We used Futura CondExtraBold at 50 points.

2 With the selection still active, choose Filter➡Blur➡Gaussian Blur (4 pixels).

3 Return to the composite channel (Command-~) [Command-~]. Choose as the foreground color a color for the marquee letters. Press (Option-Delete)[Alt-Delete] to fill the text with the foreground color.

4 Keep that selection active. Choose Filter➡Render➡Lighting Effects. Choose PlasticLightStyles (included on the CD) from the pop-up menu. If it doesn't show up in the list, see page 242 to find out how to load it from the CD. You might need to increase the Height setting to get the type as full as you want it.

The text selection should still be active, which means you could copy the text right to the clipboard or use the selection to make a path if you need to drop out the background.

VARIATIONS

If you are going to include this text in a composition, you can use the controls in the Lighting Effects dialog box to make the marquee letters appear as if they are being lit by the same light source as other objects in your composition. For this variation, we chose the Soft Direct Lights preset from the pop-up menu.

We manipulated the Five Lights Down preset to get this image.

If you deselect the text before applying the Lighting Effects filter, then the light affects the background, too. This text looks a little more like it belongs with its background.

Flip to page 174 to find out out how to create more Plastic text. ∎

1 Create a new file, and create a new channel (#4). Use the Type tool to enter the text into the new channel. This example uses Triplex Extra Bold at 100 points.

2 Use Layer➡Tranform➡Distort to give your text some dimension. If you don't want much dimension, at least stretch the letters vertically—if your letters are too short, they may turn out to be unrecognizable blobs.

3 Choose Select➡None (Command-D) [Control-D], then Image➡Adjust➡Invert (Command-I) [Control-I].

4 Apply Filter➡Brush Strokes➡ Spatter. Crank the settings up to 24 for the Radius and 15 for the Smoothness.

Your type looks pretty rough.

5 Image➡Rotate Canvas➡90° CW and Image➡Adjust➡Invert. Apply Filter➡Stylize➡Wind, with the settings at Wind and From the Left, twice.

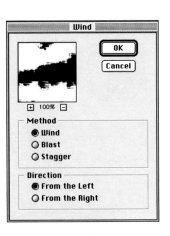

Your image looks like this.

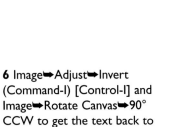

6 Image➡Adjust➡Invert (Command-I) [Control-I] and Image➡Rotate Canvas➡90° CCW to get the text back to being right-side-up.

7 Apply Filter➡Sketch➡Stamp. Set the Light/Dark Balance at 30 and the Smoothness at 13.

8 Choose Image➡Adjust➡Invert (Command-I) [Control-I], then return to the composite channel (Command-~) [Control-~]. Choose for the foreground color a dark brown. Load the selection Channel #4. Press (Option-Delete) [Alt-Delete] to fill the selection with the foreground color. Select➡None (Command-D) [Control-D].

9 To give the type a more oozy quality, use the Dodge and Burn tools to add highlights and shadows. The Dodge tool adds highlights by "under-exposing" what's painted with its tool. Burn does the opposite: It adds shadows by painting with "over-exposure." Keeping the Exposure level low (in the Burn Tool Options palette) gives greater control over the application. We used a setting of 20% here with the tone values set to Midtone. The same goes for the Burn tool.

10 To create a blobby effect, apply the Dodge tool several times in the same spot, move a short distance, and repeat. Use varying brush sizes. For this image, the brush size ranged from 25 and 45 pixels. Add shadows with the Burn tool in the same manner. A few streaks of dodging were used to connect the blobs.

11 Finally, use the Smudge tool, sparingly, to blur the blobs together a bit. That's it, and you didn't even need an oven!

VARIATIONS

Want more or less drippiness? Try varying the settings in Step 7. Here are some different results:

Molasses on a picnic table: Use Light/Dark Balance: 40 and Smoothness: 25.

Ice milk in your hands: Use Light/Dark Balance: 25 and Smoothness: 10.

Snowman in Florida: Use Light/Dark Balance: 20 and Smoothness: 5. ■

129

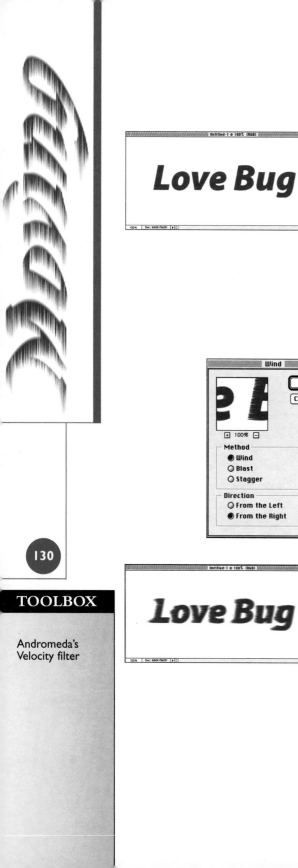

You can produce this effect using a variety of combinations of the steps that follow.

I Create a new file. Choose for the foreground color the color you want for the type. Use the Type tool to enter the text you want to use (we used Myriad Black Oblique at 50 points for this example). If you do not use an oblique font, make sure the Italic checkbox is checked. Click OK. When placing the text in the image area, be sure to leave some room to the left (or right depending on the direction you want the text to be moving). Flatten the image.

2 Apply Filter➡Stylize➡Wind (Wind, Right).

TIP To improve the dynamic of the movement use the Smudge tool to lengthen the streaks. This is not necessary, but a few touches can greatly improve this effect. Set the Smudge tool pressure to 50% and use a feathered brush.

TOOLBOX

Andromeda's Velocity filter

3 Now apply Filter➡Blur➡Motion Blur (10 pixels). You could raise this setting some, but if you go too crazy, Herbie is going to look like he's just standing there shaking.

| Motion Blur |
| OK |
| Cancel |
| ☒ Preview |
| ⊞ 100% ⊟ |
| Angle: 0 ° |
| Distance: 10 pixels |

Untitled-1 @ 100% (RGB)

Love Bug

100% Doc: 660K/563K

4 One more time, apply Filter➡Stylize➡Wind (Wind, Right).

| Wind |
| OK |
| Cancel |
| ⊞ 100% ⊟ |
| Method |
| ● Wind |
| ○ Blast |
| ○ Stagger |
| Direction |
| ○ From the Left |
| ● From the Right |

5 Apply Filter➡Sharpen➡Unsharp Mask (50, 3.5, 2) to sharpen the edges.

| Unsharp Mask |
| OK |
| Cancel |
| ☒ Preview |
| ⊞ 100% ⊟ |
| Amount: 50 % |
| Radius: 3.5 pixels |
| Threshold: 2 levels |

131

6 Next, choose Filter➡Distort➡ Shear. You can grab the line in the grid at any point and drag to make it bend. We added one point, then pulled the top and bottom points all the way to the left. Finally, we added another point on the curve to get just the bend we were looking for.

TIP **Here's another good place to use the Smudge tool to lengthen and smooth the streaks.**

7 Finally, choose Filter➡Distort➡ Spherize. We set the amount to 55.

There are many possible combinations of these steps that yield good results. You might have decided a few steps ago that you had what you were looking for.

VARIATIONS

If you're just trying to put a quick swerve in your type, then enter the text. Remember that Photoshop 4 creates the type on a separate layer, so flatten the image before you continue. Choose Filter➜ Distort➜Shear. Use the mouse to pull the center of the line out and drag the top and bottom back.

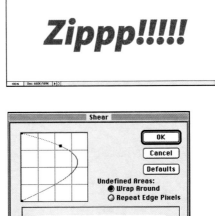

Velocity Filter

The easy way: Andromeda Software's Velocity filter was used for this effect (One-way smear, Intensity: 50, Angle: 0, Height: 50, Width: 90). ■

133

There are a number of ways to create neon using simple blurring and feathering techniques.

Quick Neon

1 Create a new file. Choose for the foreground color a bright color. Use the Type tool to enter the text. A round-edged font such as VAG Rounded Bold (80 points) works best for this effect. Flatten the image.

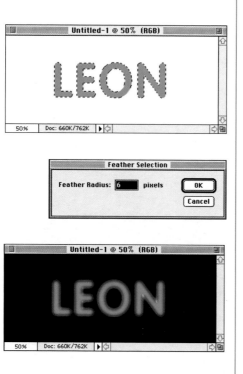

2 Use the Magic Wand tool to select the background, then Select➤Feather (6 pixels).

3 Choose black as the foreground color (press D). Press (Option-Delete) [Alt-Delete] to fill the background. That's it—short and simple.

VARIATIONS

This quick technique works well for creating handwritten neon. Create a new channel (Channel #4), then use a hard-edged brush to paint white text on a black background. Return to the composite channel (Command-~) [Control-~], and load the painted text selection (Channel #4). Fill with a color for the neon and do Steps 2 and 3.

TOOLBOX

KPT 3 Gradient
Designer

CMYK

If you are producing an RGB image, the text may look bright enough already. But if your CMYK neon looks a little dull, try this. After Step 1 save the selection. After Step 4, load the selection and choose Select➡Modify➡Contract (6 pixels, or until the selection has moved away from the edges of the text). Choose Select➡Feather (1 pixel). Now, choose Image➡Adjust➡ Curves and bend the center of the curve upward slightly, like this. This should help brighten the text.

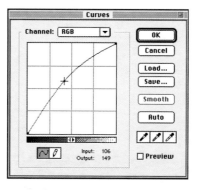

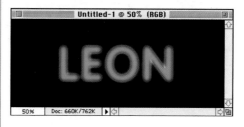

Detailed Neon

1 Create a new file. (We used a 300 dpi file for this effect.) Set the colors to the defaults (press D). Use the Type tool to enter the text. Again, we started with Vag Rounded Bold at 65 points. (Command-click) [Control-click] on the name of the new text layer to load the text selection, then save the text selection (Channel #4).

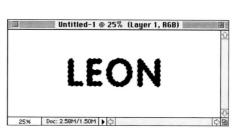

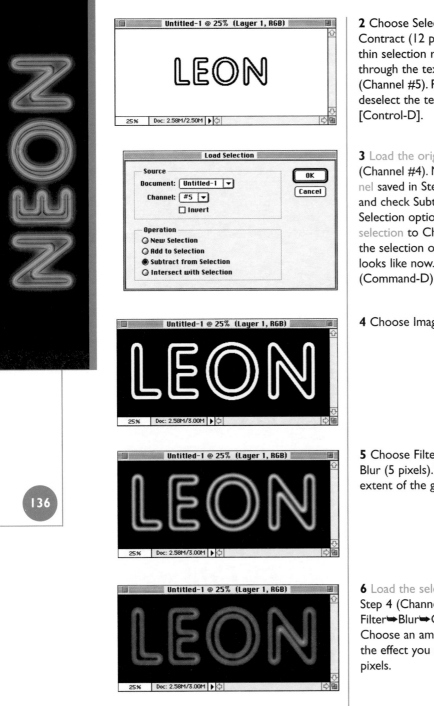

2 Choose Select➧Modify➧ Contract (12 pixels). You want a thin selection running all the way through the text. Save this selection (Channel #5). Press delete and deselect the text (Command-D) [Control-D].

3 Load the original text selection (Channel #4). Now, load the channel saved in Step 3 (Channel #5), and check Subtract from the Selection option. Save this new selection to Channel #6. This saves the selection of what your text looks like now. Deselect the tubes (Command-D) [Control-D].

4 Choose Image➧Map➧Invert.

5 Choose Filter➧Blur➧Gaussian Blur (5 pixels). This establishes the extent of the glow.

6 Load the selection saved in Step 4 (Channel #6), then choose Filter➧Blur➧Gaussian Blur. Choose an amount that matches the effect you see here. We used 8 pixels.

7 Choose Image➡Adjust➡ Brightness/Contrast (Brightness: −5, Contrast +10). The settings for your text are probably different. Find something that looks like our end result. Choose Select➡None.

TIP If you plan on printing this file and need a **CMYK** image, it's a good idea to either convert to CMYK mode or choose **View➡ CMYK Preview now. The RGB mode produces the brightest neon, but you are setting yourself up for a big disappointment when you switch to CMYK mode later.**

8 Choose Image➡Adjust➡ Hue/Saturation. Click the Colorize checkbox. The preview immediately glows bright red. Use the Hue and Saturation sliders to find a color for the neon. Try to strike a balance (with the Saturation slider) between the most intense color and the greatest amount of detail. You want a nice even color in the middle of the tubes. These are the values we used: Hue: 166, Saturation: 60, Lightness: 0.

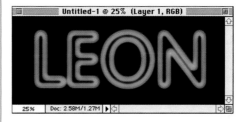

9 Load the tubes selection (Channel #6). Then choose Select➡ Modify➡Contract (4 pixels) to select a narrow line within the tubes. Choose Select➡Feather (1 pixel).

137

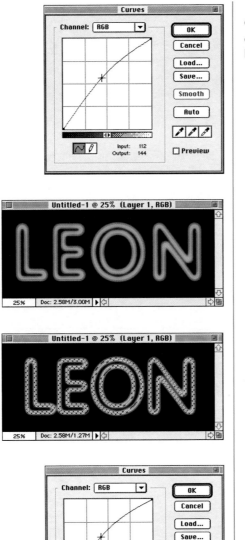

10 Choose Image➤Adjust➤ Curves, and bend the composite curve up slightly from the center, like in this figure.

11 Now choose Select➤Modify➤ Contract (2 pixels) to select an even narrower line within the tubes. Choose Select➤Feather (1 pixel).

12 Choose Image➤Adjust➤ Curves. Bend the composite curve up a little more this time.

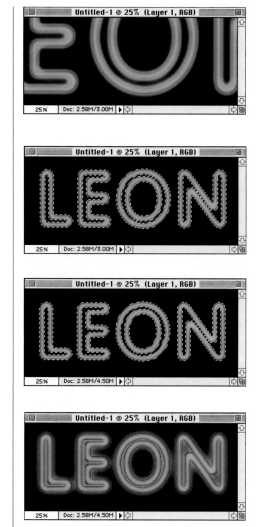

13 Load the tubes selection (Channel #6), then choose Select➡Modify➡Expand (4 pixels). The selection should now contains almost all of the glow. Save this selection (Channel #7).

14 Cut the type (Command-X) [Control-X], then fill this layer with black. Create a new layer, load the selection Channel #7 and paste it back in on the new layer.

15 Make the background layer active. The Channel #7 selection should still be active. Choose Select➡Feather (12 pixels). Choose a foreground color near the color of your text. Fill the selection. We feathered and filled the selection again in this example.

139

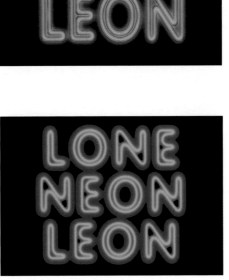

16 Add highlights to the tubes by applying the Plastic Wrap filter. Load the tubes selection (Channel #6), and choose Filter➡Artistic➡ Plastic Wrap (Highlight Strength: 6, Detail: 15, Smoothness: 10).

MORE VARIATIONS

Filters can make a quick neon easy.

KPT 3 Gradient Designer

Use the Type Mask tool to enter your type, then choose Select➡ Feather (3 pixels). Then, apply Filter➡KPT 3.0➡KPT Gradient Designer 3.0. We used one of the preset gradients for this example: True Blue Tube. Try creating your own.

Photoshop's Neon Glow Filter

Press D, then X to make the foreground color white and background color black. Choose a foreground color for the neon. Use the Type tool to enter the text. (Command-click) [Control-click] on the new layer in the Layers palette to load the type selection. Save the selection (Channel #4), then deselect the text (Command-D) [Control-D] and flatten the image. Press X. The foreground color should now be black and the background color should be the color of the text. Choose Filter➡Artistic➡Neon Glow. Finally, we loaded the text selection Channel #4, feathered it, and filled it with the neon color again. ■

OVERGROWN

142

KPT 3 Fractal
Explorer

KPT 3 Gradient
Designer

1 Create a new file. Choose a foreground color for the text. Enter the text with the Type tool, leaving enough room below the type for the overgrowth to hang down. Note that Photoshop 4 automatically creates the type in a new layer (Layer 1). Any font works well for this simple effect, but something with serifs gives the overgrowth some extra limbs to hang from. We used Cheltenham Bold at 50 points.

2 While still in the type layer (Layer 1), load the transparency selection and then immediately save the text selection to create Channel #4. Deselect the text (Command-D) [Control-D] and go to Channel #4. Duplicate Channel #4 and name the new channel Short Growth. Choose Image➡ Adjust➡Invert (Command-I) [Control-I] to invert this new channel (Short Growth).

3 Then rotate the entire image 90° clockwise (Image➡Rotate Canvas➡90° CW).

4 Apply Filter➡Stylize➡Wind (Wind, Right), then press (Command-Option-F) [Control-Alt-F] to bring the Wind filter dialog box back. Switch the direction to Left and click OK to apply it again.

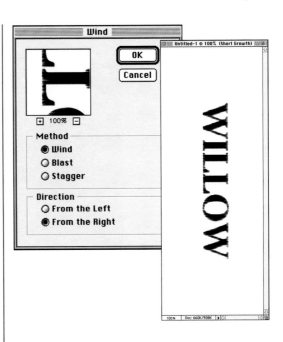

5 Press (Command-I) [Control-I] to invert the Short Growth channel. Then duplicate the Short Growth channel and rename the new channel Long Growth.

TIP You can press (Command-F) [Control-F] to apply the last filter you used with exactly the same settings. If you want to apply the filter again, but with different settings, press (Command-Option-F) [Control-Alt-F] and the dialog box from the last filter used comes up.

143

6 Press (Command-I) [Control-I] to invert the Long Growth channel. To build the overgrowth, apply the Wind filter 3 times and invert the channel again after each application. So, the dance goes like this: (Command-F) [Control-F], (Command-I) [Control-I], (Command-F) [Control-F], (Command-I) [Control-I], (Command-F) [Control-F], (Command-I) [Control-I]. Hopefully, you get something like this.

7 Choose Image➡Rotate Canvas➡90° CCW to rotate the entire image back to its original orientation. Then return to the composite channel (Command-~) [Control-~].

8 First, choose for the foreground color a color for the overgrowth. Then load the selection Channel #4. While this selection is still active, choose Select➡Load Selection, choose Short Growth from the Channel pop-up menu, and click the Subtract from Selection option.

Make sure Preserve Transparency is not checked for the Type layer, and press (Option-Delete) [Alt-Delete] to fill the new selection with the foreground color.

Load Selection

Source
Document: Untitled-1 ▾
Channel: Short Growth ▾
☐ Invert

OK
Cancel

Operation
○ New Selection
○ Add to Selection
● Subtract from Selection
○ Intersect with Selection

9 Now, load the Long Growth channel selection, and press (Option-Delete) [Alt-Delete] again to fill the new selection with the same color.

10 Deselect the active selection (Command-D) [Control-D]. To add some final touches to the drooping overgrowth, first use the rectangular Marquee tool to draw a rectangle around the extra growth beneath the text.

11 Apply Filter➠Distort➠Ripple (100, Medium).

12 Then choose Layer➠Transform ➠Perspective. Grab the lower-right corner of the perspective frame and drag it to the right. The lower-left corner moves in the opposite direction at the same rate. After you spread the overgrowth to your liking, double-click in the selection to set the perspective. Choose Select➠None (Command-D) [Control-D] and you're finished.

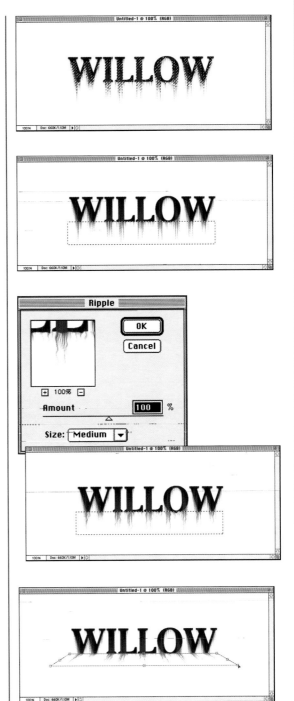

145

VARIATIONS

For our tribute to peace, love, and hair we used KPT 3 Gradient Designer and Fractal Explorer 3.0 to fill the text selection. In Step 2, after saving the selection but before deselecting the text, choose Filter➡KPT 3.0➡KPT Gradient Designer 3.0. Also, after we filled the Long Growth selection in Step 9, we shifted the selection to the right (hold down the (Option) [Alt] and (Command) [Control] keys and press the right arrow) and filled it with a different color.

You can make steam with this effect, too. We started with black text on a black background. In Step 3, we rotated the image 90° CCW instead of 90° CW. (And made sure to rotate back 90° CW in Step 7.) Then in Step 6 we applied Filter➡Stylize➡Diffuse (Normal) and Filter➡Distort➡Ripple (100, Medium). In Steps 8 and 9, we chose white as the foreground color for filling the selections. Finally, we converted the image to Grayscale mode (Image➡Mode➡Grayscale), then Duotone mode (Image➡Mode➡Duotone). The two colors I used were black and Trumatch 38-a5. ■

These techniques show you how to create text that takes on the characteristics of the surface it's painted on. The same techniques enable you to create other cool effects, too.

Painted Type

1 Create a new file, or open a file containing the background you want to put your text on.

2 Choose Select➥Select All, and copy it to the clipboard. Create a new channel (Channel #4), then paste in the clipboard.

3 The light areas of this channel represent the areas of the surface that will accept the most paint. You probably need to increase the amount of white in this channel. Choose Image➥Adjust➥Levels. Grab the right (white) Input slider and drag it to the left until the image has a good amount of white in it. Take a look at what we came up with.

4 Create another new channel (Channel #5), and use the Type tool to enter the text into this channel. We chose the Eraser Dust font (50 points). Deselect the text (Command-D) [Control-D].

5 Return to the composite channel (Command-~) [Control-~] containing your background. Make a new layer (Layer 1). Load the text channel selection (Channel #5). Then choose Select➡Load Selection, and choose the bricks channel (#4). Be sure to check the Intersect with Selection option.

6 Choose Select➡Feather (1 pixel). Choose a foreground color for the text, and press (Option-Delete) [Alt-Delete] to fill the text. To bring out more of the bricks lower the opacity of the new layer to 95%. Presto! Fresh paint without the mess.

| TIP | If the paint is too faint, you didn't give the texture channel enough white in Step 3. If it's too saturated, you gave it too much. |

Painting the Paint

If you want to paint this painted text, skip Steps 4 through 6. Instead, return to the composite channel (Command-~) [Control-~], make a new layer, and load the selection Channel #4. Choose Select➡Feather (1 pixel), and press (Command-H) [Control-H] to hide the selection edges. Lower the opacity of the new layer to around 95% before you begin painting. Choose a foreground color for the paint, and then choose the Airbrush tool (use a feathered brush with about 50% opacity). Now you can paint on the surface without completely obliterating it.

Any texture works.

149

Underpainting

The Texturizer filter (formerly part of the Gallery Effects package) is now included with Photoshop 4.0. This filter contains four textures you can paint on. We used the burlap texture for this example.

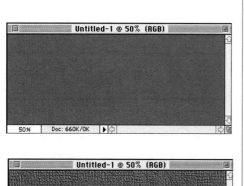

1 Create a new file and choose a foreground color for the burlap. Fill the image area with the foreground color.

2 Choose Filter➡Texture➡Texturizer and choose Burlap from the Type pop-up menu. Set the scaling to 175% and the Relief to 10.

> **TIP** If you want to paint the text yourself using the Airbrush tool, skip Steps 3 and 4, create a new layer, paint the text, and the rest of us will meet you at Step 5.

3 Create a new channel (Channel #4), and use the Type tool to enter the text into this channel. We used Brush Stroke Fast at 70 pts for this example.

4 Return to the composite channel (Command-~) [Control-~] containing the burlap background. Load the text selection Channel #4 and choose Select➡Feather (2 pixels). Choose a foreground color for the text, and press (Option-Delete) [Alt-Delete] to fill the text.

5 Keep the text selection active, and reapply the Underpainting filter (Command-Option-F) [Control-Alt-F] to get the texture to show through. To exaggerate the texture, we applied the Texturizer filter again.

Note Paper

We created a texture using the Note Paper filter for this example and used the painting method described earlier.

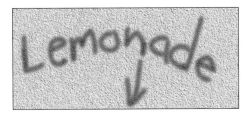

Painting with Photographs

The same techniques already discussed can be used to "paint" text with a photograph. Here are three ways to do this.

1 The first step is the same for all three. Open the file containing the photograph you want to paint with.

Use the Type Tool to Enter the Type.

2 Create a new channel (Channel #4), and use the Type tool to enter the text in the new channel. Choose Filter➡Blur➡Gaussian Blur (3 pixels) so the text has soft edges.

3 Return to the composite channel (Command-~) [Control-~], and paste in an image for the background you will paint over, or fill the image area with a color.

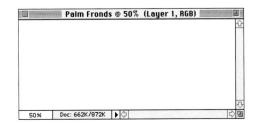

151

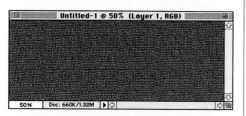

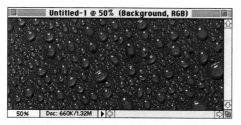

4 Load the selection Channel #4. Press Delete to reveal the photograph.

Use the Type Tool to Create Boundaries for Painting:

Do Steps 1 through 3. Double-click the Eraser tool to activate it and to open the Eraser Tool Options palette. Choose a soft brush and use the Airbrush option from the pop-up menu. (Use the Opacity slider to vary the intensity of the paint.) Load the text channel selection (Channel #4), and hide the selection edges (Command-H) [Control-H]. Start "painting" within the text. There is no need to be careful because although the selection is active, you can only affect the area within it.

If you want to mask the type inside the brush strokes, choose Select➡Inverse after loading the text selection. Now you can only paint outside the text selection.

Try filling the top layer with white.

152

Use the Airbrush Tool to Paint the Type

Do Steps 1 and 3 on page 151. Double-click the Eraser tool to activate it and to open the Eraser Tool Options palette. Choose the Airbrush option from the pop-up menu. We raised the opacity to around 75%. Now just click and paint.

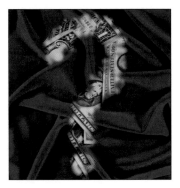

VARIATIONS

If you want to add texture to the painted photograph, copy the texture and paste it into a new channel (#4). Make sure there is plenty of white in this channel. Use the Levels (Command-L) [Control-L] dialog box if you need to add white. Return to the composite channel and make Layer 1 active. Load the selection Channel #4. Hide the edges of the selection (Command-H) [Control-H], and paint away with the Eraser tool. ■

Where can you find some really amazing patterns and textures? Just about everywhere! Check out the stock photo collections on the CD-ROM accompanying this book for some examples. There are also several commercial filters included that let you control the creation of your own textures and patterns—we've used them on the next few pages. After you create a pattern or texture you like, you can use it within your type, or even cut your type out of it. There's no limit to what you can do with these images and filters in Photoshop!

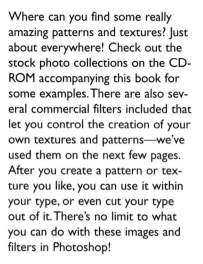

1 Create a new file. Create a new channel (#4). Enter the text, using the Type tool. We used the font Badger at 92 points with spacing of −10 for this example.

2 Open the pattern you want to fill the type with. Here we've used a custom pattern we call the Disco Frog Pattern. Select➡All and use Edit➡Define Pattern to make the entire picture into a pattern.

3 Go back into your new file, return to the composite channel, and load the selection Channel #4. Your text should be selected.

154

TOOLBOX

KPT 3 Gradient Designer

Adobe's TextureMaker (Mac only)

MicroFrontier's Pattern Workshop

Specular's TextureScape (Mac only)

Virtus' Alien Skin Textureshop (Mac only)

4 Choose Edit➡Fill and use the settings of Pattern, 100%, and Normal. This fills your text with the pattern defined in Step 3.

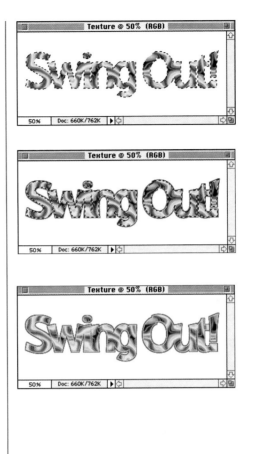

5 If you want a border around your text, choose a foreground color. We chose an obnoxious red for this example. Use Edit➡Stroke... with a setting of 3 pixels, Outside, 100%, and Normal. This puts a stroke 3 pixels wide on the outside of your selection at 100% opacity.

6 To stroke on the inside of the text, choose a different foreground color. We used yellow here. Again, choose Edit➡Stroke..., but use settings of 2 pixels wide, Inside, 100%, and Normal. This puts a yellow line on the inside of your selection. Voilà!

VARIATIONS

Bubbles

To create a texture that looks like the Lawrence Welk bubble machine just exploded, try this variation. Apply Filter➡Xaos Tools➡Paint Alchemy and use the Bubbles Grid saved style.

155

Just Plain Weird

To create really unusual textures, try Virtus' Alien Skin Textureshop. With this filter you can randomly mutate various parameters to different degrees. The results are truly wild!

To further "funkify" your text, try Filter➤Alien Skin➤Inner Bevel 2.0 along with Filter➤Alien Skin➤ Glow 2.0.

Following are some filters and programs that help you create your own textures.

TextureScape

TextureScape comes from Specular, the makers of Collage and Infini-D. This is a stand-alone application, rather than a plug-in. Its sole purpose is for creating textures and patterns...and it does so very well! If you can't find just the right texture on a stock photo CD-ROM, take a look at TextureScape!

Here, TextureScape was used to render the bark pattern, which was then imported into Photoshop for editing.

Kai's Power Tools

MetaTools offers several KPT 3 filters for creating textures. First, you could use the Gradient Designer for some pretty wild effects.

Texture Explorer is also one of the most useful tools for developing textures.

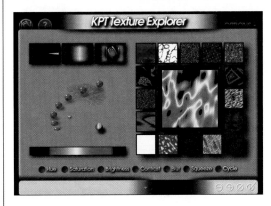

Terrazzo

This commercial filter from Xaos Tools was specifically designed to make patterns. The super simple interface makes creating patterns a snap—you can even preview the patterns as you move your cursor around the image!

We started out with this stock photo from Digital Stock.

© Digital Stock 1995

157

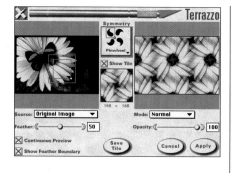

Dragging the tile around the image instantly updates the pattern preview.

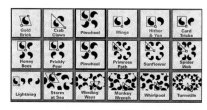

By changing the symmetry, you can create all kinds of patterns.

Adobe TextureMaker

From the architects of Photoshop comes Adobe TextureMaker, another stand-alone program designed for creating custom textures. Being able to control several lighting effects is fantastic!

Virtus Alien Skin Textureshop

This program has two flavors: a stand-alone application as well as a Photoshop plug-in. By working with the sliders under the Light …and Apply…drawer, you can create some really exciting textures.

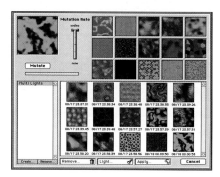

MicroFrontier's Pattern Workshop

If you like instant gratification, this is the filter for you! Pattern Workshop lets you choose from a series of premade textures in its library. This is a great plug-in if you need a texture in a hurry.

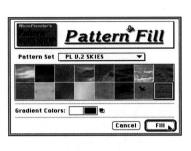

It also comes with a companion filter that lets you edit the patterns.

KPT 3 Page
Curl

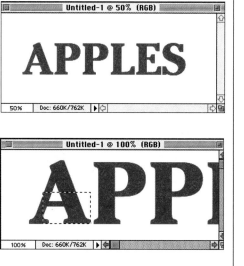

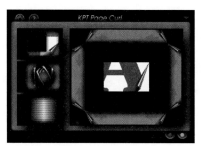

The KPT Page Curl 3.0 filter makes great curls, but it also has some limitations. The success of this technique is based almost entirely on making the right selections. So, this technique spends some time talking about selection tools. If you follow these tips, you can get the Page Curl filter to do great work for you.

1 Create a new file, and use the Type tool to enter the text. We used Cheltenham Bold at 70 points for this example. Save the selection (Channel #4). You may not need the selection, but it's better to have it on hand just in case.

2 The KPT Page Curl filter uses the foreground color as the color it places underneath the peel-away type. So choose as the foreground color a color for the surface. (Note: The color fills in the entire area within the selection and to the right of the curl.)

The Easy Way

To use this filter you must first make a selection. In most cases, you want to make simple rectangular selections. Inside a rectangular selection, the KPT Page Curl filter peels the type away from the bottom right (unless you change the settings).

The angle of the top of the flap follows an imaginary line from the top-right corner to the bottom-left corner of the selection rectangle. This selection (made with the rectangular Marquee tool) yields this result after applying Filter➡KPT 3.0➡Page Curl 3.0.

This is not what you want because it looks like the background is peeling up, too. The top right corner needs to be on the right edge of the text, so make a selection such as this…

…to get this.

Now you can select the Paintbrush tool and paint over the leftover pieces of text.

This figure shows the selection we made for the P.

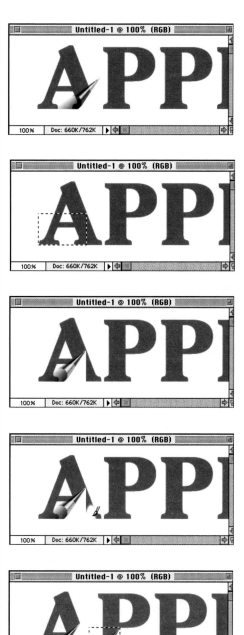

161

APPLES

You could render the entire text with the method above (which is what we did to create this figure), but if you want more control, check out what we did next.

More Control

To get more control you have to make some irregular selections. Use the rectangular Marquee tool to make this selection.

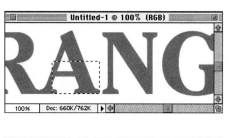

If you have a selection active and hold down the (Option) [Alt] key while making a second selection, the new selection area is subtracted from the active one. Select the Lasso tool. Start outside the active selection and cut into it along the contour of the text, like this.

Now, apply Filter➡KPT 3.0➡Page Curl 3.0 to get this.

The only problem is the funny edge
on the top of the curl. Press
(Command-Z) [Control-Z] to undo
the curl. Again hold down the
(Option) [Alt] key, and draw a ring
to clip off the corner of the selection, like this.

Apply Filter➡KPT 3.0➡Page Curl
3.0 again to get this.

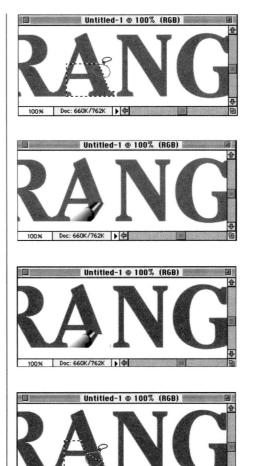

If you took too much of the selection away and came up with this...

...you can hold down the Shift key
instead of the Option key to add a
new selection to the active selection to get this.

Then apply Filter➡KPT 3.0➡Page
Curl 3.0 to get this.

TIP If you want the tops of all
the peels to come up to
the same point, turn on the
Rulers (Command-R)
[Control-R] and pull down
a guide from ruler at the
top of the window to the
point where the tops of
your selections should be.

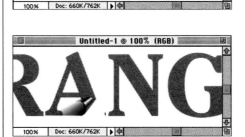

163

ORANGES

So, build the type one curl at a time. First, make the selection, then apply Filter➤KPT 3.0➤Page Curl 3.0. It's really very simple after you get used to what the KPT Page Curl filter is going to do with your selection. You don't have to be satisfied with one peel per letter, either. Here is the final type.

VARIATIONS

Darken the Peel

If you want to darken the curl and make it more opaque, then reapply the filter and adjust the opacity setting in the KPT Page Curl dialog box. You can get something to look like this.

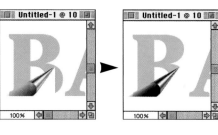

Torn Peels

You can use the selection technique described in the previous section, "More Control," to make the text look like it's been torn. When you use the Lasso tool, cut further down into the text.

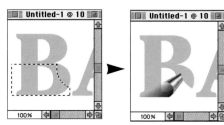

More Peels

First, choose the same foreground color as the type color. Then, after applying the Page Curl filter, keep the selection active, and select the rectangular Marquee tool. Hold down the (Option) [Alt] and Shift keys while drawing a box starting from the lower-right and moving to the upper-left. Stop before you draw the box over the entire original selection.

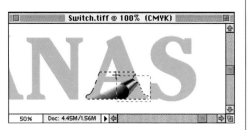

Use the Lasso tool as described in "More Control" to subtract any parts of the selection, and apply Filter➡ KPT 3.0➡Page Curl 3.0. Before making the last peel, choose the same foreground color as the color of the image's background (white in this case).

Switch Directions

If you want the text to peel up from another direction, just click and drag on the arrows in the KPT Page Curl filter to choose your direction.

Color Underneath

If you want the Page Curl filter to insert a color under the areas of the letters that were lifted, first choose that color as the foreground color. Next, load the type selection Channel #4 (saved in Step 1). Then hold down the (Option) [Alt] and Shift keys and draw a selection with the Lasso tool around one of the letters. Now only that letter is selected. Use the Marquee tool as described in the "More Control" section to make the proper selection for the letter. You probably need to subtract the top half of the letter from the selection. In the case of a letter such as an A, you need to add to the selection the space between the legs of the A so the filter has some space to put the curl. ■

Photoshop's Layer➡Transform features can be used by themselves to quickly add dimension to your type, or they can be a useful aid in layering type onto preexisting surfaces.

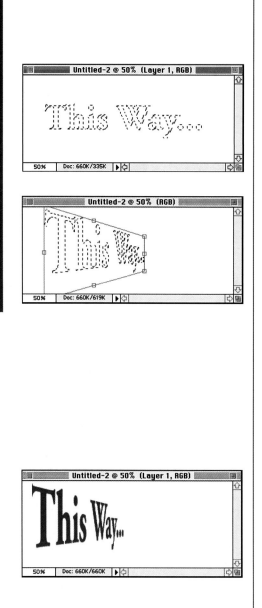

1 Here's the way the perspective feature works. Create a new file, and use the Type Mask tool to enter the text. We began with Cheltenham Bold at 50 points.

2 While the text selection is still active, choose Layer➡Transform➡ Perspective. A box appears around the type. You can use the square tabs on the corners of the box to reshape the box. When you move one of the tabs, another tab (the one that's along the same line as the direction of your movement) moves at the same rate and along the same line but in the opposite direction. It sounds a little confusing, but as soon as you try it you'll understand. The result is that the text is either compressed or expanded at one end, creating the illusion that it's receding in space.

3 Press (Return) [Enter] key to set the text as you see it, or press Escape to cancel the perspective transformation. This is what you end up with if you press (Return) [Enter] and then fill the selection with purple.

4 You can have the perspective move in any direction you want.

Placing Text On a Receding Surface

1 We opened a stock photo of a mailbox from CMCD for this example. Using the perspective feature helped put Santa's name on the box.

2 Use the Type tool to enter the text (15-point Cheltenham Bold). Remember, font size is important to make this look authentic. Also, we used the Eyedropper tool to select a color for the type from the mailbox flag. The type is on a new layer (Layer 1). This enables us to make changes to the type without affecting the background image of the mailbox.

3 The quickest way to lay type on a flat, receding surface such as this mailbox is not to use the Perspective feature, but rather the Skew feature. Position the type so that the first letter is in place, as in the previous figure, then choose Layer➡Transform➡Skew. A box appears identical to the box used in the Perspective feature.

167

4 If you move one of the corner tabs, the tab you move toward moves away in the same direction, creating a parallelogram. After you release the tab for the first time, however, the tabs act independently of all the others. So, first we grabbed the tab on the upper right and moved it upward until the top line of the Skew box was in line with the lines near it on the mailbox.

5 Then we moved the lower-right tab upward to compress the text and make it appear as if it was receding. Press (Return) [Enter] when you're finished.

6 The next two steps help blend the text into the side of the mailbox. First, find the Opacity slider on the Layers palette and lower the opacity in Layer 1 (the type layer) to 90% to allow some of the mailbox to blend with the colored type.

7 Next, create a layer mask for Layer 1. In the layer mask, choose Filter➡Noise➡Add Noise (Uniform). Before pressing Return you can watch the type in the image window change as you adjust the noise Amount, which we set at 80. Click OK, flatten the image, and you're finished.

VARIATIONS

The perspective feature was used
to create this type, before adding
the drop shadow. See page 199 to
find out how to create the shadow.

■

Here is a soft 3-D look with a crimp around the edges.

1 Open a new file, and create a new channel (#4). Choose black as the foreground color and white as the background color. Use the Type Mask tool to enter the text in the new channel. We used Futura Bold at 100 points in this example.

2 We began with a typeface that had hard edges, so we chose Select➡Modify➡Smooth (5 pixels) to round the edges. If you choose a nice rounded typeface to begin with, you can skip this step.

3 Press X to switch the foreground and background colors. Choose Edit➡Stroke (2 pixels, Outside, 50% Opacity, Normal). Press (Option-Delete) [Alt-Delete] to fill the selection with white.

4 Choose Filter➡Blur➡Gaussian Blur. The amount depends on the thickness of your text. We chose 8 pixels. Then choose Image➡ Adjust➡Brightness/Contrast and raise the contrast until you see some black move in around the edges. We raised the contrast to 25.

5 Choose Image➡Adjust➡Levels (Command-L) [Control-L], and slide the Output Levels right (white) slider to the left until the box above it reads about 200.

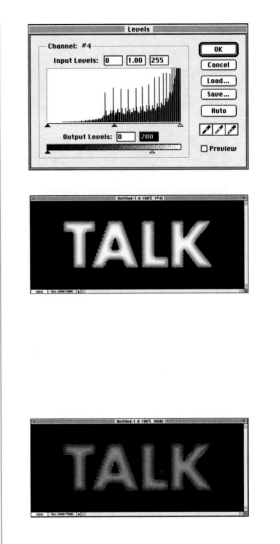

6 Now, to fluff the pillow. Choose Filter➡Stylize➡Find Edges. If the text is too contrasty after applying the Find Edges filter, then you probably raised the contrast too high in Step 4. You can use the Levels dialog box (Image➡Adjust➡Levels) to adjust the values in the text.

7 Return to the composite channel (Command-~) [Control-~]. We filled the background with black to get the shiny text to stand out. Load the selection Channel #4.

8 Choose the foreground color for the text. Press (Option-Delete) [Alt-Delete] to fill the text.

171

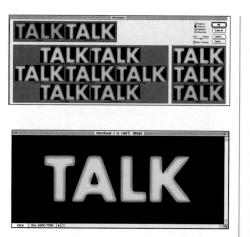

9 You may think the text looks a little dull. Choose Image➡Adjust➡ Variations and use the previews to monitor your alterations.

Then choose Image➡Adjust➡ Brightness/Contrast and bump the contrast up again to 25. You may need to experiment with the settings. You could also fill the text twice by pressing (Option-Delete) [Alt-Delete] a second time in Step 8.

TIP Don't forget that hiding the active selection gives you a better, unobstructed view of what your text really looks like. Press (Command-H) [Control-H] to hide the selection marching ants, and press it a second time to make them reappear.

VARIATIONS

To add a slight glow and softness to the text, after Step 9, with the selection still active, choose Edit➡Stroke (2 pixels, outside, 50% opacity, normal).

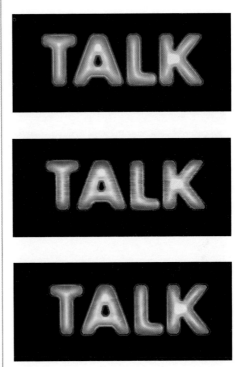

To add some texture to the text, choose Filter➡Stylize➡Wind (Wind, Left). Then apply the same filter (Command-Option-F) [Control-Alt-F], but change the settings to Wind and Right.

For this variation, we created a new layer and loaded the selection Channel #4 and pasted a colorful image into the selection. Then we chose Color from the blending mode pop-up menu. ■

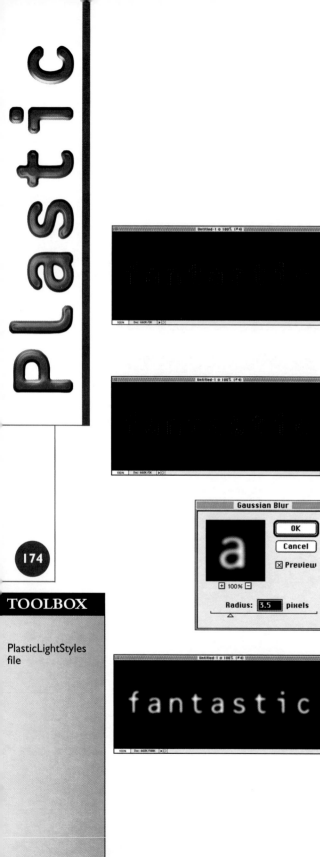

This task takes advantage of Photoshop's Lighting Effects filter. Included on the CD-ROM is a lighting styles file that contains the presets for this effect. If you want to use this preset file, consult Appendix A, "What's On the CD-ROM," to find out where to put it on your hard drive.

1 Create a new RGB file. (It must be an RGB file in order for the Lighting Effects filter to work.) Create a new channel. Change the foreground color to black and the background color to white. Use the Type Mask tool to enter your text. We used OCR-B at 50 points in this example.

2 If you want to give your text some smoother corners choose Select➡Modify➡Smooth (3 pixels).

3 Fill the text with white by pressing Delete. Deselect the text (Command-D) [Control-D]. Choose Filter➡Blur➡Gaussian Blur (3.5 pixels).

174

TOOLBOX

PlasticLightStyles file

4 Load the selection of the same channel you are working in (Channel #4). Choose Filter➡ Blur➡ Gaussian Blur. Blur the text until you get something resembling what you see in this figure. You should be able to see highlights and dark areas. Deselect the text (Command-D) [Control-D].

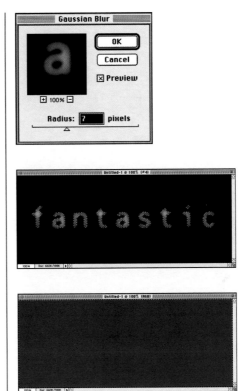

5 Return to the RGB window (Command-~) [Control-~]. Select a foreground color near the complement of the color you want the text to be. We used a blue for the red-orange text we wanted to make. Fill the image with this color (Option-Delete) [Alt-Delete].

6 Choose Filter➡Render➡Lighting Effects, and choose PlasticLight-Styles from the pop-up menu or match the settings seen in this figure. The circular ring surrounding the light source should encompass your text. Click and hold on one of its handles and drag to resize it.

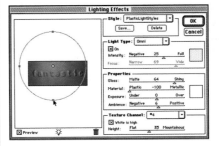

175

7 Load the same selection you did in Step 4 (Channel #4). Choose Image➡Adjust➡Hue/Saturation (Command-U) [Control-U], click the Colorize checkbox, and use the Hue slider to choose the color of your text. We also slid the Lightness slider to −19. Depending on your color choices you also might want to lower the Saturation.

8 You might also want to open the Levels dialog box now (Command-L) [Control-L] and adjust the Input Levels to fine tune the plastic. Moving the right (white) and middle (gray) sliders to the left helps brighten the image.

TIP To select the letters without the background, load the selection **Channel #4. Choose Select➡Modify➡ Expand. The amount depends upon the typeface you are using. We used 6 pixels in this example.**

VARIATIONS

To bring out more ridges in the plastic (like you see in the "Plastic" thumb tab), before deselecting the text in Step 4, choose Image➡ Adjust➡Brightness/Contrast, and try these settings: Brightness −33, Contrast +13. You are trying to bring out some light and dark areas within the text selection. Continue with the rest of the steps above. We also increased the saturation as a final step.

For a quick embossed plastic, you can skip Step 4 and stop after Step 6. We opened a stock photo from Digital Stock for this example and also skipped everything in Step 5, except returning to the composite channel.

The Chrome section contains a variation that uses the steps above to create a chrome look like this. See page 48 for details on creating Chrome type. ■

© Digital Stock 1995

177

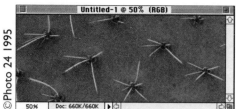

This type effect is great for making your type look as though it pops out of the background. It's a really quick and dirty technique!

1 Create a new file or open up an existing image. We used a stock photo from Photo 24 (cropped, obviously) from the CD.

2 Create a new layer (Layer 1) for the text. Use the Type Mask tool to enter the text. Be sure that you're in the text layer (Layer 1), not the background layer. We used the font Hobo at 100 points for this example.

3 Save the selection (#4).

4 Select➡Feather and use a setting of 3 pixels. Change the foreground color to black. Change to the Gradient tool and set the options to Transparent to Foreground, Linear, and 100% opacity. Drag the Gradient tool, top to bottom, about [1/3] of the way down the selection. You should get something such as this.

5 Now load the saved selection (#4). Using the Marquee tool, move the selection up and to the right with the arrow keys until there's a thin line of black on the bottom and left sides of the selection.

6 Press Delete to remove what's in the selection and Select➡None. If you need to reposition the shadow, simply use the Move tool. The underlying background is not affected.

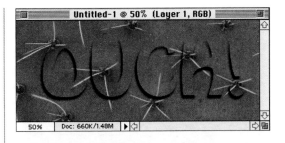

To make the text look like it's popping up even more, after Step 4, use the Layer➡Transform➡Skew command and skew the shadow's bottom to the left. Continue with Step 5. ■

© Digital Stock 1995

1 Open the file containing the image onto which you want to reflect your type.

2 Use the Type tool to enter the text. The text is placed on a new layer (Layer 1). Move the type into position with the Move tool (press V, and then use the arrow keys).

3 Click the text layer (Layer 1) and drag it to the New Layer icon in the Layers palette. This creates a new layer (Layer 2) for the reflection.

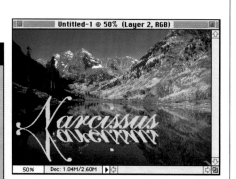

4 Choose Select➡All (Command-A) [Control-A]. Choose Layer➡ Transform➡Flip Vertical, then drag the flipped type down (while holding the Shift key to make sure it moves straight down) until the bottoms of the letters touch each other.

180

TOOLBOX

Andromeda's
Reflection filter

5 Choose Layer➡Transform➡Scale and pull the bottom of the scale box up to squeeze the text vertically. Press Return to set the scaling. Load the reflection layer's transparency selection and save this selection (Channel #4), then deselect the type (Command-D) [Control-D].

6 On the Layers palette, slide the Opacity down to around 45%. This number varies depending on how dark your text is and how dark the surface is. It's that simple to make the reflection. The rest of the steps are for fine tuning.

> **TIP** You may find that switching to either **Soft Light** mode or **Overlay** mode works better for your text. If you do switch to one of these modes, keep the Opacity higher.

7 Choose Layer➡Add Layer Mask➡Reveal All. The Layers palette should now look like this.

8 Now use the rectangular Marquee tool to select the reflected type and a small area around it.

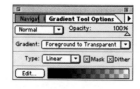

9 Double-click the Gradient tool to select it and to open the Gradient Tool Options palette. Choose the Foreground to Transparent option from the style pop-up menu. The gradient Type should be set to Linear. Choose black as the foreground color (press D then X).

10 After you make the gradient, the bottom of the reflection fades into the surface. Click near the bottom of the rectangular selection and drag toward the top, about two thirds the height of the word. You should now see something like this.

11 Make Layer 2 active. Now, choose New Layer from the Layers palette menu and keep the selection active.

12 Make sure the foreground color is set to black (or another dark color). Use the Gradient tool with the same options as you set up in Step 9. Click near the middle of the original text and drag (while holding the Shift key) a short way into the reflected text to create a shadow.

13 To distort the text, because ours was underwater, we hid all layers except Layers 2 and 3 and chose Merge Visible from the Layers palette menu. After the layers were merged, only Layer 2 remained, with a Blending mode of Normal (rather than the Soft Light or Overlay mode you may have changed it to after Step 6).

14 With the rectangular selection around the reflected type still active, apply Filter➡Distort➡Ripple (100, Large) to supply the final touch.

VARIATIONS

Andromeda's filters contain a Reflection filter that makes reflections much easier, but only in certain situations because the area surrounding the type is also reflected. (If you select the type only, then the filter has no area in which to place the reflection.) The Filter➡ Andromeda➡Reflection dialog box enables you to control 5 characteristics of the reflected type, and gives you a preview.

This checkerboard stock photo from Fotosets already had a slight reflection. We added the type (from the Chrome section, see page 48) and made its reflection match the already existing one. ∎

Background: © Fotosets 1995

Rough Edges

There are countless Photoshop and third-party filters that can be used by themselves or in combinations to add rough edges to your text. The following pages contain demonstrations of what some of the third-party filters can do. But first, here are a few combinations we came up with by using only Photoshop's built-in set of filters.

Set-Up

Create a new file, and use the Type tool to enter the text. You could also use any type that you rendered with another technique and want to embellish. This type is Frutiger Bold at 45 points.

Photoshop Filters

Apply Filter➡Distort➡Ripple (100, Large), then apply Filter➡Distort➡Ripple (500, Small).

Apply Filter➡Pixelate➡Mosaic (6 pixels).

Apply Filter➡Pixelate➡Fragment.

Apply Filter➡Pixelate➡Fragment, then Filter➡Distort➡Ripple (100, Medium).

Mosaic

Mosaic

Mosaic

Mosaic

TOOLBOX

Xaos Tools'
Paint Alchemy
(Mac only)

Apply Filter➡Pixelate➡Fragment, Filter➡Distort➡Ripple (100, Medium), and Filter➡Stylize➡Find Edges.

Apply Filter➡Pixelate➡Mosaic (6 pixels), Filter➡Stylize➡Find Edges, and Image➡Adjust➡ Threshold (255).

Apply Filter➡Distort➡Ripple (300, Medium), and Image➡Adjust➡ Brightness/Contrast (Contrast: +50).

Apply Filter➡Distort➡Wave (Type: Triangle; 1 generator; Wavelength: 2, 40; Amplitude: 10, 10; Scale: 100, 100; Wrap Around).

Apply Filter➡Distort➡Wave (Type: Square; 1 generator; Wavelength: 2, 20; Amplitude: 10, 10; Scale: 50, 50; Wrap Around), and Filter➡ Distort➡ Ripple (200, medium).

Displace Filter

Inside the Adobe Photoshop➡ Plug-ins folder is a folder named Displacement Maps. In this folder, Adobe has supplied some ready-made displacement maps. Test them all if you have the time, or consult your Photoshop manual to see how you can make your own.

Deselect the text (Command-D) [Control-D], and apply Filter➡ Distort➡Displace (Horiz.: 7, Vert.: 7, Tile, Repeat Edge Pixels).

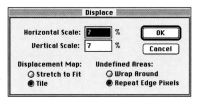

Mosaic

A dialog box appears and asks you to find a displacement map. Find the Displacement Maps folder mentioned above. We chose the Crumbles file for this example. You can use the same technique to create all the type variations on this page.

In the Displace dialog box, we entered 10 for both the Horizontal and Vertical settings, and switched to the Stretch to Fit option. Then we chose the Mezzo effect displacement map.

To the last figure we applied Filter➡Stylize➡Diffuse (Darken) three times for this result.

Mosaic
Mosaic
Mosaic

The Horizontal and Vertical settings were both set to 7 (Stretch to Fit), and we used the Rectangular tiles (10%) displacement map.

We (Command-clicked) [Control-clicked] the new type layer in the Layers palette to select the type. Then we changed the Horizontal and Vertical settings in the Displace dialog both to 5. Finally, we used the Schnable Effect displacement map.

Photoshop 4 comes with a set of filters full of features to help you roughen the edges of the text. These used to be called Aldus's Gallery Effects filters.

186

Here is the Spatter in action.

Here is Ripple.

Rough Pastels with Canvas chosen as the texture.

Water Paper and some hairy extensions.

A slight fuzz provided by Conte Crayon.

Paint Alchemy

Xaos Tools' Paint Alchemy is a perfect Photoshop plug-in for roughening the edges of text. There is a working version of Paint Alchemy 1.0 on the CD-ROM, and a demo version of Paint Alchemy 2.0. We used version 1.0 to create these type treatments. Here is what the interface for Paint Alchemy 1.0 looks like.

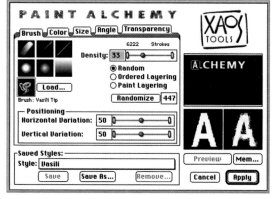

187

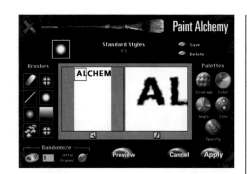

And this is the Paint Alchemy 2.0 interface:

Use the Type tool to enter the text, then deselect it (Command-D) [Control-D], and choose Filter➡ Xaos Tools➡Paint Alchemy 1.0 (or Paint Alchemy 2.0). Your options in this interface are endless. If you use the preset styles, you probably need to make adjustments so that only the edges of your text are affected. After you find an effect you like, click the Randomize button then the Preview button to see variations of the same settings. Here are some treatments we discovered.

For this one, we chose the preset Vasili from the Abstract Styles sub-menu in the Paint Alchemy dialog, then adjusted the settings to affect only the edges.

This one began with the Cotton Ball preset from the Misc. Styles submenu in the Paint Alchemy dialog.

Mosaic

Mosaic

To create this one we started with the Pointillist preset from the Misc. Styles submenu in the Paint Alchemy dialog box. Then we used Image➡Adjust➡Brightness/Contrast to increase the contrast.

For the last one here we began with the Screen Mosaic preset from the Misc. Styles submenu in the Paint Alchemy dialog box. ■

Mosaic

Mosaic

189

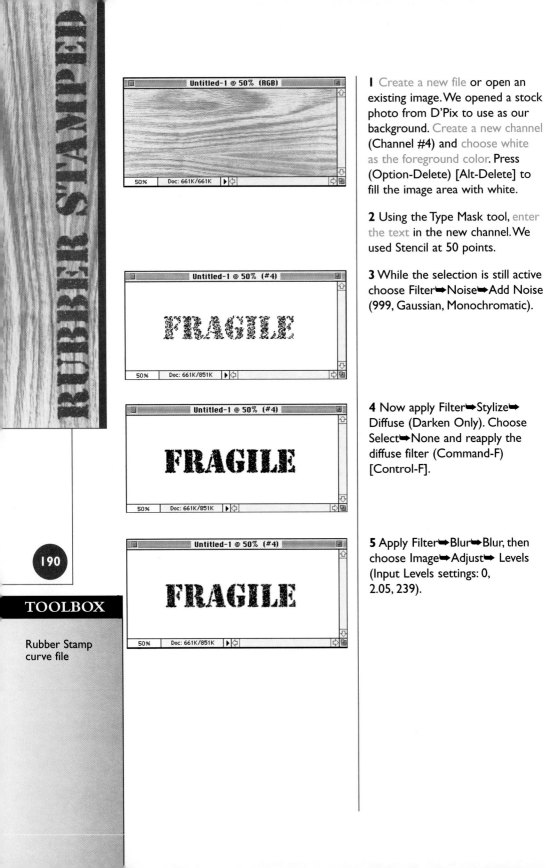

TOOLBOX

Rubber Stamp
curve file

1 Create a new file or open an existing image. We opened a stock photo from D'Pix to use as our background. Create a new channel (Channel #4) and choose white as the foreground color. Press (Option-Delete) [Alt-Delete] to fill the image area with white.

2 Using the Type Mask tool, enter the text in the new channel. We used Stencil at 50 points.

3 While the selection is still active choose Filter➡Noise➡Add Noise (999, Gaussian, Monochromatic).

4 Now apply Filter➡Stylize➡ Diffuse (Darken Only). Choose Select➡None and reapply the diffuse filter (Command-F) [Control-F].

5 Apply Filter➡Blur➡Blur, then choose Image➡Adjust➡ Levels (Input Levels settings: 0, 2.05, 239).

6 Now choose Image➡Adjust➡ Curves (Command-M) [Control-M]. Click the Load button and find the Rubber Stamp curve, or bend the curve up just like you see it here. Press (Command-I) [Control-I] to invert the channel.

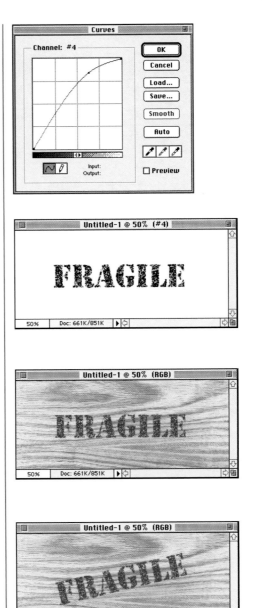

7 Return to the composite channel and load the selection Channel #4. Choose red as the foreground color and press (Option-Delete) [Alt-Delete] to fill the selection. Fill it a second time for stronger ink. You can experiment with the Opacity slider for a more realistic effect.

8 Now deselect the text (Command-D) [Control-D], rotate the type selection (Layer➡Transform➡Rotate), and it's ready to ship.

191

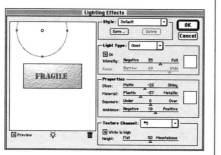

VARIATIONS

Here's another ink-stamped effect, that is more heavily stamped as if someone had used too much ink on the pad. Complete all the preceding steps, with these exceptions:

4 Skip this step.

5 After blurring the text, choose Filter➡Noise➡Median (3 pixels). Finish this step, and all the others, too.

To incorporate a paper texture with the ink, we first built the text (using all the steps except Step 8) in a new file. Then we applied the Note Paper filter (Filter➡Sketch➡ Note Paper) to an empty white channel (#5), returned to the composite channel, and chose Filter➡ Render➡Lighting Effects. We chose the Note Paper channel (Channel #5 for us) as the Texture Channel and set the Height to 50. We used a white Omni light and moved it far enough away that it wouldn't shine too harshly on the paper surface.

Now see what happens when you apply the Note Paper filter to the final image with these settings: Image Balance: 25; Graininess: 10; Relief: 13. ■

Basic Drop Shadow

1 Create a new file, choosing white for the background color in the New File dialog box, or open a file containing a background for your type.

2 Choose a foreground color for your type, and use the Type tool to enter the text. We made this groundhog with 50-point Cheltenham Bold type. Rename this layer Type. Load the type selection by (Command-clicking) [Control-clicking] the Type layer.

3 Create a new layer, name it Shadow, and drag the layer so it becomes the layer directly below the Type layer. Make the Type layer invisible so you can see the Shadow layer—just a blank white screen in our case.

TOOLBOX

Alien Skin's Drop Shadow filter

KPT 3 Gradient Designer

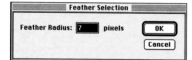

4 The text selection should still be active. Choose Select➡Feather (7 pixels). The higher the feather radius, the more diffused the shadow. Choose a foreground color for the shadow color, and fill the selection. Deselect the shadow selection (Command-D) [Control-D].

TIP **Black is the most common color for shadows, but choosing black doesn't mean that the shadow won't have any color. If the shadow is black and you lower the opacity of the layer, the color from the background will show through the shadow.**

5 Make the Type layer visible again, but keep the Shadow layer as the active one. The Layers palette will look like this.

6 Use the Move tool to move the shadow out from underneath the text. Then use the Opacity slider on the Layers palette to control how strongly the shadow covers the background. The Shadow layer opacity in this example is 90%. Now you have a basic drop shadow.

Shadows on Images

If you are placing the text on top of an image and want a more realistic shadow that takes the background image into account, then do Steps 1 and 2 and continue with these steps:

3 Select the Marquee tool and drag the selection slightly away from the type. The selection will move, but your type should stay where it is. Choose Select➡Feather (7 pixels).

4 Now, make the Background layer active. Press Command-J to create a layer by copying the selected area of the background. The floating selection will become this new layer. Rename this new layer Shadow.

5 Now that you have the background copied into the Shadow, you can alter it with any of Photoshop's tools. For this example, we chose Image ➡Adjust ➡Hue/Saturation (Hue: –115, Saturation: –65, Brightness: –49), and set the Shadow layer mode to Multiply. For a soft shadow set the mode of the Shadow layer to Multiply in the Blending Mode pop-up menu on the Layers palette. Or try colorizing the shadow with the Image➡Adjust➡Hue/Saturation Colorize option.

VARIATIONS

Adding a Glow

Make the Shadow layer the active layer. (Command-click) [Control-click] the Shadow layer to select the shadow. Make a new layer. Drag the new layer so that it becomes the layer directly below the Shadow layer. Choose Select➡Modify➡ Border (15 pixels, Outside). Choose a foreground color for the glow, and press Option-Delete to fill the selection. Press Option-Delete two or three more times to intensify the glow.

KPT 3 Gradient Designer

This multicolored drop shadow was created using KPT 3 Gradient Designer to fill in the shadow in Step 4 of the Basic Drop Shadow technique.

Alien Skin Drop Shadow 2.0 Filter

A much easier way to create a drop shadow is to use the Drop Shadow filter from Alien Skin's Eye Candy collection, formerly called Black Box (included on the CD). Just enter the text in the composite channel. Choose the foreground color you want to use for the drop shadow. Load the selection, choose Filter➡Alien Skin➡Drop Shadow 2.0.

197

Perspective Shadows

Creating a perspective shadow is virtually the same as creating a drop shadow. You only need to distort the shadow so that it looks like it's falling back on a surface. Complete Steps 1 through 3 of the Basic Drop Shadow section (except don't hide the Type layer), then continue with these steps:

4 Fill the selection with white. (You won't see any change when you fill the selection because the Type layer is on top of the Shadow layer.)

5 Since our shadow is coming forward we first had to flip it, and then align it. Choose Layer➡Transform ➡ Flip➡Vertical, then drag the flipped text down until the bottoms touch.

6 Photoshop has several distortion tools useful for creating the right form for the shadow, but the most versatile is the Distort command. Choose Layer➡Transform➡ Distort. You can now drag the four corners of the selection in any direction you want. We dragged the bottom two corners down and to the left. Press the Return [Enter] key when you're satisfied.

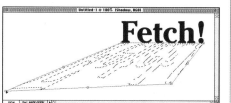

7 Now we have the shape for the shadow, but before filling it we're going to fade the near edges of the text. Press Q to enter Quick Mask mode. Double-click the Gradient tool to select it and open the Gradient Tool floating palette. Make the settings as you see them in this figure, and choose black as the foreground color.

8 Click the bottom of the shadow with the Gradient tool and drag straight up about one-third of the way through the shadow. You should see something like this in Quick Mask mode.

TIP Holding the Shift key while dragging the Gradient tool keeps the gradient straight.

9 Press Q to exit Quick Mask mode. Choose Select➡Feather (2 pixels) to soften the selection. Choose a foreground color for the shadow. Press Option-Delete to fill the shadow.

To create this floating type, the original text was distorted with the Image➡Effects➡Distort transformation (as described in the Perspective Shadow steps above), then we followed the Basic Drop Shadow steps on page 194. ■

ShatterMap file

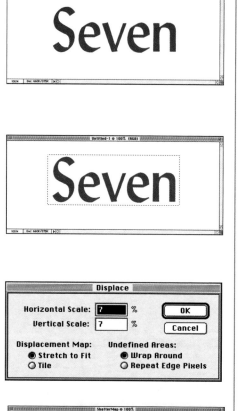

This is your one-step guide to shattered type. For this effect, I've done all the work for you.

1 Create a new file, and use the Type tool to enter the text. We used Lydian at 60 point. You may want to increase the letter spacing in the Type dialog box to give the letters some room for splintering. If you want a more concentrated shattering effect, leave the spacing alone. Flatten the image.

2 Use the rectangular Marquee tool to select an area surrounding the type. Grab some of the surrounding area, but not too much.

3 Choose Filter➡Distort➡ Displace. Use these settings: Horizontal Scale 7, Vertical Scale 7, Stretch to fit, Wrap Around. Click OK.

4 A dialog box appears asking you to choose a displacement map. Find the ShatterMap preset file from the CD-ROM. This file is a grayscale displacement map that we created. It shifts parts of the image (or text) according to the lightness or darkness in areas of the displacement map. Although you won't see this figure, we wanted to show you what the displacement map looks like.

5 Click OK, and that's it. If the displacement map distorts your text too much or too little, either adjust the size of the area you select around the text in Step 2 or adjust the values in Step 3.

VARIATIONS

For this variation, we applied the Displace filter a second time with the same displacement map and the same settings.

Before flattening the image in Step 1, load the transparency selection of the type layer. We opened a stock photo from D'Pix, copied it, returned to our text file, and chose Edit➡Paste into.

First, we rendered the type using the Marquee effect on page 124, then followed Steps 2 through 4 to create this type. ■

201

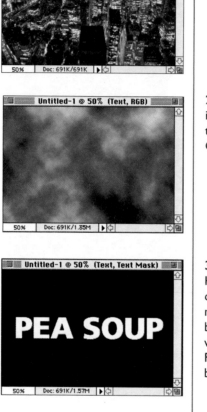

Depending on how you use this effect, it can also look like fog.

I Create a new file or open a file containing the image you want to place the foggy or smoky text over.

2 Create a new layer, and rename it "Text". Make the Text layer active, then choose Filter➡Render➡ Clouds.

3 Create a layer mask for this layer. Hold the (Option) [Alt] key and click on the layer mask, so only the mask is visible. Fill the mask with black and enter the text in white with the Type tool. We used Frutiger Black at 50 points, with bold applied.

202

TOOLBOX

KPT 3
Gaussian f/x

4 Choose Image➡Rotate Canvas➡ 90° CW, then Filter➡Stylize➡ Wind (Wind, Right). Reapply the filter (Command-F) [Control-F].

5 Choose Image➡Map➡Invert (Command-I) [Control-I]. Apply the Wind filter two more times (Command-F, Command-F) [Control-F, Control-F], and invert the image again (Command-I) [Control-I]. Rotate the image back (Image➡Rotate Canvas➡90° CCW).

6 Now apply these filters: Filter➡ Distort➡Ripple (–50, Large), Filter ➡Blur➡Motion Blur (20°, 10 pixels), Filter➡KPT 3.0➡KPT 3.0 Gaussian f/x. You may also use the KPT 2.1 Gaussian Electrify filter instead. You may want to apply the Gaussian filter two or three times.

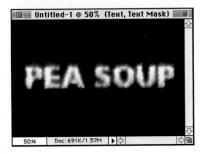

203

TIP If you (Option-click) [Alt-click] again on the Text layer mask to make everything visible, you can see that you now have a smoky text. A shortcut to a whiter foggy text is to choose Image➡Adjust➡ Brightness/Contrast and raise both the Contrast and the Brightness. For more subtle variations, follow the rest of the steps.

7 Create a new layer (rename it "Clouds"). Then create a layer mask for this layer, and choose Filter➡Render➡Clouds.

8 Hold down the (Option) [Alt] key and use the mouse to position the hand icon over the line that separates the Text layer from the Clouds layer. When the hand turns into an icon that looks like INSERT fog.mask.icon, click on the line. This makes the Text layer act as a mask for the Clouds layer.

VARIATIONS

These variations give you some minor adjustments you can use to make your type look a little better.

Use the Smudge tool to improve the look of the smoke or fog. If you click on the layer mask for the Text layer to make it active, you can use the Smudge tool on the text while viewing the results to the entire image without affecting the other layers. Set the Smudge tool Pressure to 50%.

If you want to strengthen the text, then make the Clouds layer mask active and choose Image➡Adjust➡Brightness/Contrast and raise the Contrast. You can also do this to the Text layer window. If raising the Contrast is too harsh, then try adjusting the Levels (Command-L) [Control-L].

You probably noticed that after Step 7 and before Step 8, clouds were floating in front of the entire image. If you like that effect, but want the text to stand out more, then stop after Step 7 and choose Image➡Adjust➡Brightness/Contrast. Raise the Contrast all the way to 100, and slide the Brightness slider either all the way up or all the way down.

Add some color to the text by selecting a foreground color after creating the new layer in Step 2, or filling the Clouds layer with a solid color instead of white. ■

TOOLBOX

EmbossLighting
Styles file

Adobe Illustrator

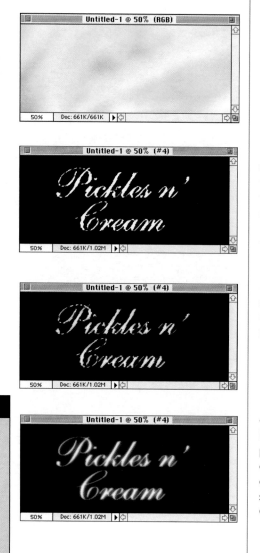

This effect uses the extremely pow-erful Lighting Effects filter. Included on the CD-ROM are several preset LightingStyles files to be used with this filter. To find out what you need to do to load these files, turn to page 241 in Appendix A, "What's On the CD-ROM."

1 Create a new file, or open a file containing the background that you want to stitch. Whatever you use, it must be an RGB file in order for the Lighting Effects filter to work.

2 Create a new channel (Channel #4). Use the Type tool to enter the text in the new channel. This effect was created with a script font, such as Shelley Andante (which we used here at 70 points), in mind. Save the type selection in another new chan-nel (Channel #5).

3 Return to Channel #4 (if neces-sary), and choose Filter➡Blur➡Gaussian Blur (3 pixels) to blur the inside of the text selection only.

4 Choose Select➡Inverse, then Filter➡Blur➡Gaussian Blur (5.5 pixels) to blur only the outside of the text selection. Now, you can get rid of that annoying active selection (press Command-D or Control-D).

5 Choose Filter➡Stylize➡Find Edges.

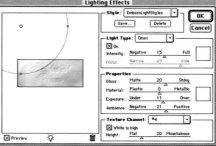

6 You are building a grayscale texture channel to be used with the Lighting Effects filter. Right now, things are a bit too harsh for a stitched-on-silk look. Choose Image➡Adjust➡Brightness/Contrast and use settings near these: Brightness 22, Contrast –46.

7 For a final softening choose Filter➡Blur➡Gaussian Blur (1 pixel).

8 Return to the composite channel (Command-~) [Control-~] where the innocent silk awaits your cruel puncturing. Choose Filter➡ Render➡Lighting Effects. If you loaded the LightingStyles files, choose EmbossLightStyles from the styles pop-up menu. If you haven't loaded it, then use the settings you see in this figure.

You should see something like this.

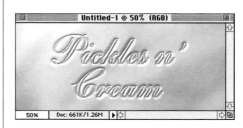

207

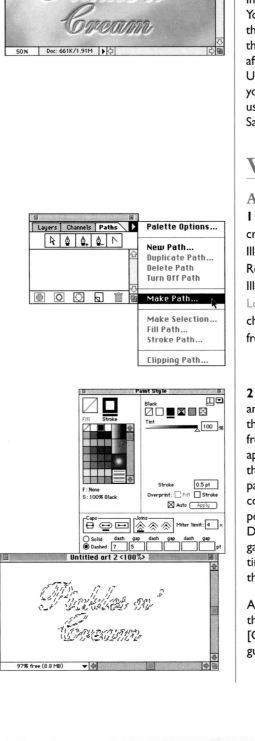

9 To change the color of the type, load the selection Channel #5 (the original type selection), and choose Image➤Adjust➤Hue/Saturation. You may or may not want to check the Colorize checkbox. If you don't, then the Hue slider is only going to affect the darker areas of the type. Use the sliders to find the color you want. Here are the settings we used for this example: Hue: 95, Saturation: 74, Lightness: –42.

VARIATIONS

Adding Stitches

1 We used Adobe Illustrator to create the stitches. Open Adobe Illustrator, and open a new file. Return to Photoshop while Illustrator runs in the background. Load the selection Channel #5, and choose Make Work Path (1 pixel) from the Path palette menu.

2 Copy the path to the Clipboard and switch to Adobe Illustrator. On the empty page, paste in the path from the Clipboard. The path appears in Illustrator. Do not lose the selection. In the Paint Styles palette, choose black for the stroke color. Make the stroke weight 0.5 points. Switch the line style to Dashed with a 7 pt. dash and a 5 pt. gap. Make the ends round. Your settings should match what you see in this figure.

And the text path should look like this (press (Command-Shift-H) [Control-Shift-H] to hide the blue guides).

3 Copy the path to the Clipboard (Command-C) [Control-C]. Return to Photoshop. Choose Turn off Path from the Paths palette menu. Load the selection Channel #5, and paste in the Clipboard (Command-V) [Control-V]. A dialog box appears; choose Paste as Pixels (anti-aliased) and click OK.

4 Press (Command-H) [Control-H] to hide the edges. You can see the stitches are black now. If you want to change their color or soften them, Choose Image➡Adjust➡ Hue/Saturation. We checked the Colorize box for this example and used these settings: Hue: 180, Saturation: 100, Lightness: +16.

More Stitches

If you want to make the stitches look more raised, after Step 7 complete Steps 1 through 3 of Adding Stitches with one exception: choose white as the stroke color in Step 2. Deselect the stitches (Command-D) [Control-D] and finish Steps 8 and 9. The image should now include a row of indentations that gives the impression of stitches.

To add color to More Stitches, load the stitches selection Channel #6. Hold down the (Command and Option) [Control and Alt] keys and press the up arrow and left arrow once. Then choose Select➡Feather (1 pixel). Choose Image➡Adjust➡ Hue/Saturation. We used these settings: Hue: −25, Saturation: 100, Lightness: 0. ■

209

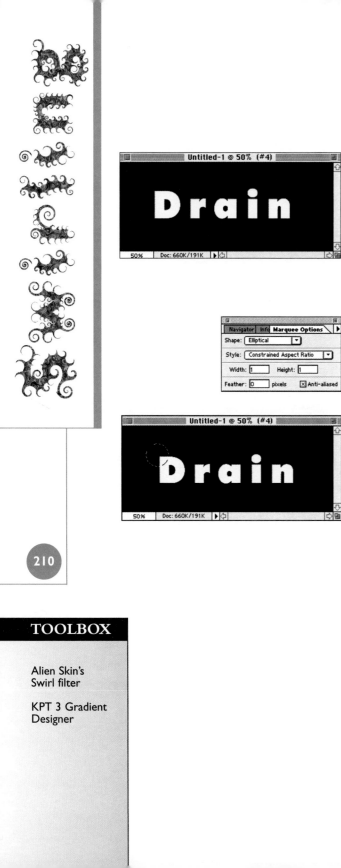

This effect will take some patience—and a lot of trial and error. Save often and get friendly with the Undo command!

1 Create a new file, and create a new channel. Choose white as the foreground color and black for the background color. Use the Type tool to enter your text into the new channel. We used Futura Extra Bold at 60 points for this example, with the spacing set at 12 to provide some extra room between the letters.

2 Change the Marquee tool shape to Elliptical and the Style to a Constrained Aspect Ratio with Width: 1 and Height: 1. This gives you a perfect circle.

3 Select a part of one of the letters, keeping the body of the letter less than halfway through the circle. If part of the letter goes over halfway through the circle, the result is the background bleeding into the letter rather than a spike coming out of the letter (just try it…you'll see what we mean). If you need to move the marquee, but don't want to change the size, just drag the selection. Only the marquee moves—not what's in it!

210

TOOLBOX

Alien Skin's
Swirl filter

KPT 3 Gradient
Designer

4 Choose Filter➡Distort➡Twirl. Move the slider until you like what you see in the preview window. If you can't get what you want, cancel and move the selection a bit or try using a different size selection. Both of these changes can have profound effects on the filter.

Now you have the first one.

5 Move the selection or make a new one and continue swirling until you have a finished product.

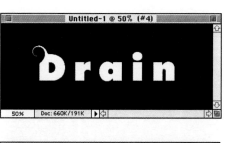

6 Return to the composite channel ((Command-~) [Control-~]) and fill the area with any color or texture you want to appear in your type. We used a texture from Kai's Power Tools and applied Filter➡ Alien Skin➡Swirl 2.0 (Spacing: 22, Length:7, Twist: 90, and Detail: 100). (Warp and Smooth were checked too.)

211

50%   Doc: 660K/850K

7 Load the selection. Channel #4 and Select➡Inverse (or you could have clicked the Invert box in the Load Selection dialog box.) Press Delete to fill the selection with white. You're left with the letters filled with a pattern!

VARIATIONS

You can treat your swirled type just as you could anything typed with the Type tool, meaning you can apply a barrage of other effects from this book. Try some Neon, for instance (page 134) we feathered the selection 3 pixels, then used KPT Gradient Designer's Gradient on Paths option with a custom gradient.

Or try Flaming (page 80). A few extra swirls really add to that "hot" effect, don't they? ■

Although it is possible to create type that looks three-dimensional within Photoshop, there are several other applications that make this task a lot easier. On the CD are demo versions of a few of these three-dimensional rendering applications, including: Adobe Dimensions, Infini-D, and StrataType 3d. There is also a demo version of Andromeda Software's 3-D Photoshop filter. This technique uses Dimensions to model some 3-D type, then uses Photoshop to dress it up.

1 Open Adobe Dimensions 2.0. A new document window opens. Press (Command-E) [Control-E] to make sure that you are working in Edit mode, where everything runs faster. Then choose Operations➡ Extrude (Command-Shift-E) [Control-Shift-E]. The Extrude floating palette appears onscreen. Click the New Base button on the palette.

2 A new untitled window appears onscreen, and the icons in the tool-bar change. Double-click the Type tool to select it and open the Character palette. Make your selections in the Character palette. We used 100-point Bodoni Ultra Bold for this example.

3 With the Type tool, click in the Extrude window that opened in Step 2. A cursor appears. Type in the text.

TOOLBOX

Adobe
Dimensions
(Mac only)

KPT 3 Texture
Explorer

TIP If you want beveled type, then see **Steps 3, 4, and 5 in the Beveled type section on page 30**, then skip to **Step 5 of this section.**

4 Find the Extrude floating palette. Enter, in points, the depth you want the text to extrude. We used a value of 25 points. We also chose the end caps option. Click the Apply button on the Extrude floating palette.

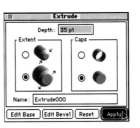

5 To go back to the original image window choose Window➡ Untitled-1. Now you can see that the text has been extruded. What you see is actually a wireframe model of the type. Before rendering the final image, you need to set its color.

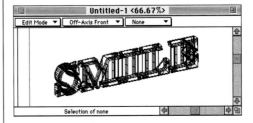

6 Choose Appearance➡Surface Properties. A floating palette appears. The figure here explains its features. For the Fill (text) color, we used these CMYK values: 0/95/80/0. For the Shade (shadow) color, we used black. We left the Stroke (edge) color at none. Click the Reflectance icon, then the Plastic icon, and use the values shown in the figure. Click the Apply button when you're finished.

215

7 To show off more of the perspective of the type, we selected View➡Custom Perspective and set the angle to 115°. Then we moved the type straight down so the perspective would affect the type even more.

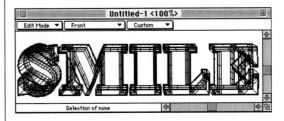

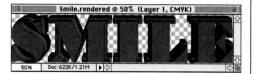

8 You won't see any changes in the text because you're not in a render mode yet. Choose View➡Shaded Render. (Complex type may take some time to render, depending on your system configuration.) If you don't like what you see, you can simply use the Surface Properties palette to make appearance changes, or go back to the Extrude palette and use the Edit buttons to alter the text. Remember, it's always quicker to work in Edit mode (View➡Edit Mode).

9 When you are satisfied with the type, deselect the type (Command-Shift-A) [Control-Shift-A], and choose File➡Export. Choose Color Macintosh and Adobe Illustrator 5 from the pop-up menus in the Export dialog box. Quit Dimensions. No need to save changes—you already exported what you wanted.

10 Open Photoshop, and open the file you just exported from Adobe Dimensions. Here are the settings we used in the Rasterizer box.

11 The text opens into Layer 1 and there isn't a background layer. The image is complete and ready for you to embellish with Photoshop.

12 The rest of the steps demonstrate how to map a pattern onto the 3-D type. First duplicate Layer 1 to make Layer 1 copy. Then, choose Luminosity from the Layers palette blending mode pull-down menu.

13 Make Layer 1 active, and Select➡Load Selection (Layer 1 Transparency) to select the outline of the type. While the selection is active, fill the selection with white.

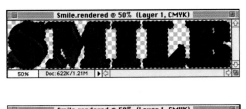

14 Add a texture to jazz up the type, if you want; we used KPT Texture Explorer. Then flatten the image.

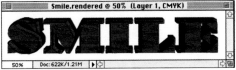

TIP To map a stock photo texture onto the type, open the photo, select the area you want to use, copy it to the Clipboard (Command-C) [Control-C], and close the file. In Step 13, instead of filling the text with white, choose Edit➡Paste Into.

Type on a 3-D Surface

Adobe Dimensions is also a valuable tool for placing flat type on a three-dimensional surface.

1 Again, open Adobe Dimensions 2.0. A new window appears. The toolbar includes tools to create boxes, spheres, cones, and cylinders. We decided to put our type on a sphere. Click the Sphere tool on the Tool palette to select it, then use the crosshairs to draw a box in the Untitled-1 window area. To make a perfectly round sphere, hold the Shift key to keep all the dimensions the same.

217

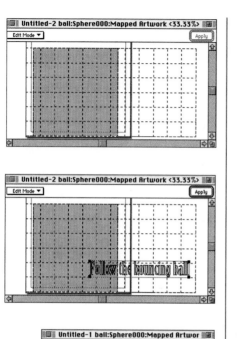

2 Choose Appearance➡Map Artwork (Command-Option-M). A new window opens and the tools in the toolbar change. The grid in the new window is a "map" of the sphere. The gray areas are the areas of the sphere hidden from view in the Untitled-1 window.

3 Double-click the Type tool to select it and open the Character floating dialog box. Type in the text, press Return, then move the text where you want it on the map.

4 Press (Command-Y) to see a preview of the text only. To change the fill or stroke color of the text, press (Command-I) to open the Surface Properties floating dialog box.

TIP If you want to edit the type while still in the Map Artwork window, go back to the Edit mode (Command-E) and use the Type tool to select the text and the floating Character dialog box to make any changes.

5 Click the Apply button in the upper-right corner of the Map Artwork window, then choose Window➡Untitled-1 to see the type mapped onto the sphere.

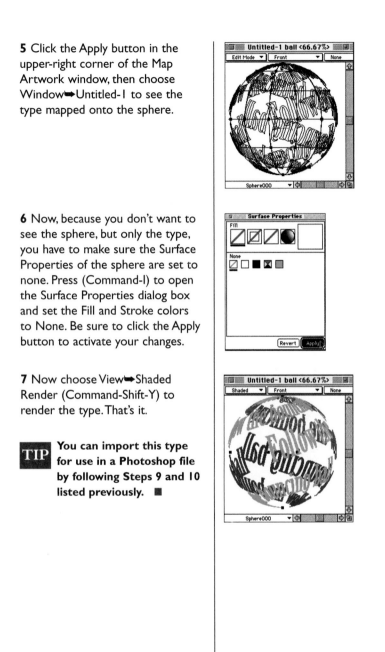

6 Now, because you don't want to see the sphere, but only the type, you have to make sure the Surface Properties of the sphere are set to none. Press (Command-I) to open the Surface Properties dialog box and set the Fill and Stroke colors to None. Be sure to click the Apply button to activate your changes.

7 Now choose View➡Shaded Render (Command-Shift-Y) to render the type. That's it.

TIP You can import this type for use in a Photoshop file by following Steps 9 and 10 listed previously. ■

Photoshop's layer features make this one a breeze. By placing the type on a layer on top of the background images, we can adjust the opacity and experiment with many different effects without actually affecting either layer permanently.

1 Open the file containing the background you want to lay the type over. We used a stock photo from Digital Stock here.

©Digital Stock 1995

2 Choose white as the foreground color. Use the Type tool to enter the text.

3 To make this type transparent, all you have to do is lower the opacity of this new layer.

Grab the Opacity slider in the Layers palette and slide it to the left.

VARIATIONS

This technique is so simple it gives you lots of time to experiment.

To make the text a little brighter in this image, we chose Overlay from the Layers palette blending mode pop-up menu.

You don't have to keep the text white. For this variation, we made the text 100% cyan and chose Screen from the pop-up menu.

221

Another quick way to work with this effect is to create a new channel (#4) and type the text into it. Then return to the composite channel and load the selection Channel #4. You can now manipulate the selection any way you like. In this variation, we chose Image➡Adjust➡Brightness/Contrast, and bumped the brightness all the way up to 100. Use the Levels sliders (Image➡Adjust➡Levels) for more control.

You can also knock words out of a transparent overlay. First, in a new layer above the background photo, we filled a box with white and lowered its opacity. Then after creating each word with the Type Mask tool, we pressed Delete.

If you want a foggy or smoky transparency, flip to page 202 and take a look at the Smoke technique. ■

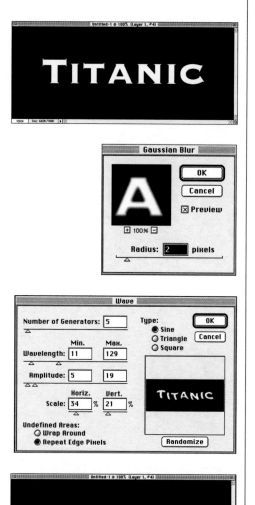

1 Create a new file, and create a new channel (Channel #4).

2 Use the Type tool to enter the text in the new channel. We used Copperplate 33 BC at 70 points in this example.

3 Use Filter➡Blur➡Gaussian Blur (2 pixels) to soften the edges of the text.

4 Apply Filter➡Distort➡Wave (Type: Sine; Generators: 5; Wavelength: 11, 129; Amplitude: 5,19; Horiz.: 34%; Vert.: 21%).

Click the Randomize button a few times until the thumbnail has a watery look to it (this randomizes settings based on the values you entered). Your text should look something like this.

224

5 To make the shadow, duplicate Channel #4. In the new channel (#5) select the text with the rectangular Marquee tool. Use Layer➡ Transform➡Distort to offset and warp the text a little more (remember, this will be a shadow so you may want to move the layer around a little).

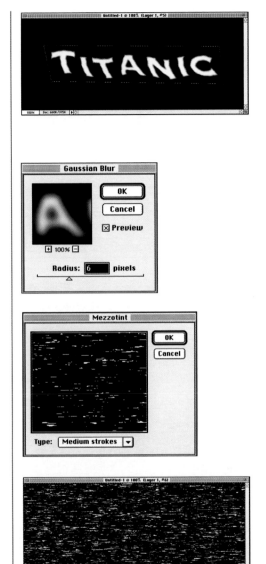

6 Use Filter➡Blur➡Gaussian Blur (6 pixels) to blur the shadow channel. Drop the selection ((Command-D) [Control-D]).

7 For the water, create a new channel (Channel #6). Apply Filter➡Pixelate➡Mezzotint using the Medium strokes option. Repeat this two more times (press (Command-F) [Control-F] twice).

Channel #6 should now look something like this.

225

8 Apply Filter➡Blur➡Gaussian Blur (4 pixels).

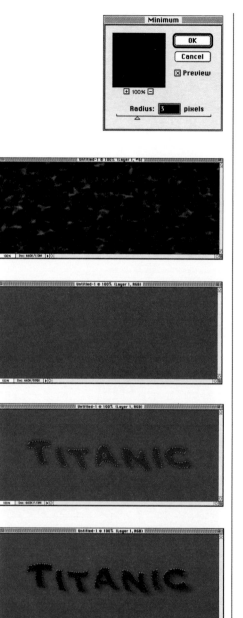

9 Apply Filter➡Other➡Minimum (3 pixels.) This creates the spider-web look for sunlight shimmering on the water.

10 Choose Image➡Adjust➡ Brightness/Contrast and adjust the settings to get something like this.

11 Now it's time to create the visible image. Return to the composite Channel. Choose a foreground color for the water. We used a medium cyan color here. Press (Option-Delete) [Alt-Delete] to fill the entire image with the chosen color.

12 Load the selection Channel #5 (the shadow channel). Choose for the foreground color a medium blue color for the shadow. Press (Option-Delete) [Alt-Delete] to fill the selection.

13 Use Select➡Load Selection to load Channel #4 (the text channel). Set the foreground color to the color you want the text to be. Here we used a forest green. Press (Option-Delete) [Alt-Delete] to fill the selection.

14 Load the selection Channel #6 (the highlight channel). Choose white as the background color and press Delete to fill the selection. Don't lose the selection yet!

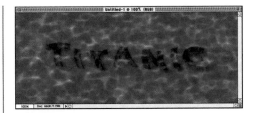

15 To add a few more highlights, apply Filter➡Artistic➡Plastic Wrap with the settings Highlight Strength: 20, Detail: 13, Smoothness: 15. Don't worry what the preview looks like—it doesn't take into account the various levels of your selection.

Presto! Don't forget to breathe!

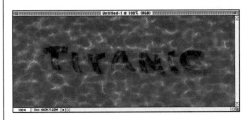

VARIATIONS

To create the watery text without the background, follow Steps 1 to 10. Then,

11 Load the selection Channel #5 to load the shadow channel. Choose for the foreground color a color for the shadow. Here we used cyan. Press (Option-Delete) [Alt-Delete] to fill the selection. If the shadow isn't dark enough, press (Option-Delete) [Alt-Delete] again as we did here.

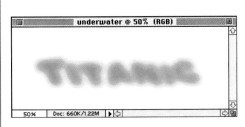

TITANIC

12 Load the selection Channel #4 to load the text channel. Choose a foreground color for the text be. We used a dark blue color. Press (Option-Delete) [Alt-Delete] to fill the selection.

13 Load the selection Channel #6 to load the highlight channel. Choose white as the background color. Press Delete to fill the selection. If you want the highlights brighter, press Delete again. (Using the Plastic Wrap filter causes some dark streaks in the large white areas of the image which are much more noticeable on white than on a colored background.) ■

TOOLBOX

Xaos Tools'
Paint Alchemy
(Mac only)

StripesForVDT
file

This effect works best if you intend to use it for onscreen display. In other words, if you are going to use it as an RGB image. You just can't get that glowing green color in a CMYK image.

1 Create a new file. Choose black as the foreground color (press D), and press (Option-Delete) [Alt-Delete] to fill the image with black.

2 Create a new channel (#4), choose Filter➡Render➡Texture Fill, and load the StripesForVDT file from the *Type Magic* CD-ROM. Or, create the stripes yourself: First, use the rectangular Marquee tool to select the left half of the new channel, and fill the selection with white. Then choose Filter➡Distort➡ Wave (Type: square; Generators: 1; Wavelength: 1, 50; Amplitude: 999,999; Horiz.: 100; Vert.: 0). Be sure to choose the Repeat Edge Pixels option. Choose Filter➡ Other➡Maximum (amount: 1) to fatten the white stripes and thin down the black stripes.

TIP Use the upper-limit value of the Wavelength in the Wave filter to control the thickness of the lines if you are using a different size type. If you increase this value, then slightly increase the value used when applying the Maximum filter to this channel.

3 Create another new channel (#5) and use the Type Mask tool to enter the text you want to use. We used 90-point Compacta Bold for this effect.

4 To find the intersection of the stripes with your text, Command-Option-Shift-click [Control-Alt-Shift-click] the Channel.

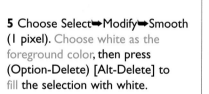

5 Choose Select➡Modify➡Smooth (1 pixel). Choose white as the foreground color, then press (Option-Delete) [Alt-Delete] to fill the selection with white.

231

6 Choose Filter➡Blur➡Gaussian Blur (5 pixels). Deselect the type (Command-D) [Control-D].

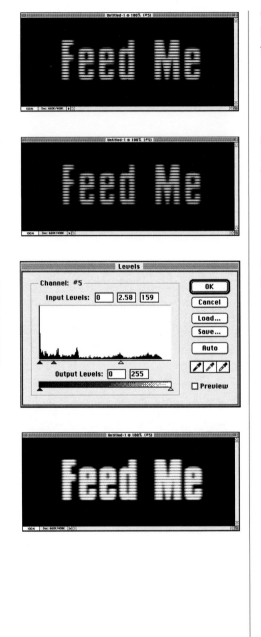

7 Choose Image➡Adjust➡ Brightness/Contrast and raise the contrast to 25.

8 Choose Filter➡Blur➡Motion Blur (Angle: 0; Distance: 10). Choose Filter➡Blur➡Gaussian Blur (1 pixel).

9 Choose Image➡Adjust➡Levels (settings: 0, 2.58, 159).

10 (Command-~) [Control-~], and choose a foreground color. Here, we used R: 0, G: 255, B: 0. Load the selection Channel #5 (the blurred text). Press (Option-Delete) [Alt-Delete] two or three times to fill the selection to the desired brightness.

TIP	**If you plan on using this text as a CMYK file, you should convert to CMYK mode (Mode➡CMYK Mode) before selecting the foreground color. That way you won't be shocked when you convert to CMYK mode and find all the brightness stripped from your otherwise-glorious VDT text.**

11 Press (Command-D) [Control-D] to deselect the text. A final blurring finishes it off. Choose Filter➡Blur➡ Gaussian Blur (1 pixel).

VARIATIONS

Apply Filter➡Xaos Tools➡Paint Alchemy (Video Styles➡Blue Video). The Gilded CD font was used for these examples.

If green is your favorite color, color the type black and apply Filter➡Xaos Tools➡Paint Alchemy (Video Styles➡Green Video). That's all there is to it. ■

PlasticLightStyles
file

I Open a file containing a cement background. The file must be in RGB format because this effect uses the Lighting Effects filter. We used a stock photo of stucco which you can find in the D'Pix folder.

2 Create a new channel (#4). Use the Type tool to enter the text. Use a font that looks like it has been handwritten or distort the text to make it look handwritten. Deselect the text (Command-D) [Control-D].

3 Duplicate Channel #4 (#5). In the new channel, choose Filter➡ Stylize➡ Diffuse (Lighten Only). Press (Command-F) [Control-F] four or five times to re-apply the filter.

4 Load the selection Channel #4 (the text selection). Choose Filter➤Blur➤Gaussian Blur (4 pixels).

5 Press (Command-I) [Control-I] to invert the area within the selection. Choose Brightness/Contrast and raise the Brightness to about 55 and the Contrast to 20. Deselect the text (Command-D)[Control-D].

6 Return to the composite channel. Choose Filter➤Render➤Lighting Effects. Choose the PlasticLight-Styles from the pop-up menu. Choose Channel #5 for the texture channel, change the Height to about 45. To move the light so it doesn't wash out the type, click it in the preview and drag it to its new location.

TIP If the PlasticLightStyles does not appear in the menu, then you need to load it into your Adobe Photoshop folder. See Appendix A, "What's On the CD-ROM", on page 241 for more info.

237

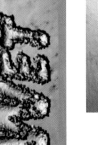

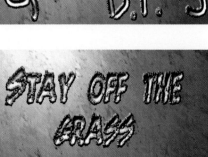

VARIATIONS

To make the text look more hand-written, use the Paintbrush tool to draw the letters. Choose a hard-edged brush and follow the rest of the steps.

Try using a rougher font such as Brush Stroke Fast. Before deselecting the text in Step 5, choose Filter➡Stylize➡Diffuse (Lighten Only). Reapply the filter (Command-F) [Control-F], deselect the text (Command-D) [Control-D], do Step 6, and you're done.

If you want to make a mess, before deselecting the text in Step 5, choose Filter➡Stylize➡Find Edges. Follow Step 6. Make Channel #5 active, set the Magic Wand tool Tolerance to 10, and use it to click in the white area surrounding the text (also, hold the Shift key and click in white areas in the middle of letters such as O and Q). Return to the composite channel. Choose white as the foreground color and press (Option-Delete) [Alt-Delete] to fill the selection with white. ▪

Appendix A

What's On the CD-ROM

The CD-ROM that comes with this book is both Macintosh and Windows compatible. Please note that there are several demos and tryouts available for Macintosh users that are not available for Windows users, and vice versa. This means that either the product does not exist for that platform, or a version is being created but was not available at the time of publication.

We suggest that you refer to the READ ME and other information files included in the demo software program's folder. Also, visit the corporate Web sites for updates and more information. (The URLs are noted in Appendix B.) There are often demos of new software available for downloading and tryout.

The CD-ROM is divided into six folders. Macintosh folder names are in parentheses, and Windows folders are in brackets.

Contents

(Type Effect Preset Files) [TEPF]

This is a collection of ready-to-use files listed in the Toolbox section of techniques in the book. You'll need to install and refer to these files when creating certain type effects.

(Effects) [EFFECTS]

This is a collection of effects for manipulating images in Photoshop. Featured is a sampler of edge effects from AutoF/X.

(Filters)

This folder contains lots of different filters you can use to manipulate your images. You can do a variety of things with filters, one of the most powerful features of Photoshop. Some of these filters are freeware, some are shareware, and some are commercial demos.

(Fonts) [FONTS]

Here you will find an excellent selection of shareware fonts to use in the various type effects.

(Images) [IMAGES]

You'll need some high-quality images to use as backdrops for some of the type effects described in the book. This collection of images from various commercial stock photo companies will give you plenty to play with.

(Software) [SOFTWARE]

This folder contains demos of commerical software, including Adobe products, Specular LogoMotion and Equilibrium DeBabelizer—plus much much more.

Installation

For detailed instructions on how to install and use the resources we've included on the CD-ROM, please consult the READ ME or ABOUT files in the individual software, filter, effects, and imagery folders. General installation information follows:

Filters

Filters should be copied into the Plug-Ins folder, located in the same place as your Adobe Photoshop application. Then, restart your computer, relaunch Photoshop, and find the filters in the Filter menu. You can now access and apply these third-party filters the same way you use Photoshop's filters.

Preset Files

Before installing the type effects preset files, we recommend you first create a new folder to hold all the presets *except the lighting styles files*. It is *extremely* important that you remember to put the lighting styles files (all named with "LightingStyles" after the effect's name) in the Photoshop➡Plug-Ins➡Filters➡Lighting Effects➡Lighting Styles folder with the other Photoshop lighting styles, otherwise they will not work.

The other preset files we have provided can be opened via the Select a Document dialog box. To bring up this box, you can either choose File➡Open or wait till Photoshop automatically opens it for you, as in the Liquid effect when you choose Load Settings in the Curve dialog box to load LiquidCurve. In either situation, you'll open the Photoshop folder on your hard drive, find the preset folder you created at the start and select the preset file you'd like.

Fonts (Macintosh)

Fonts should go in the Fonts folder, located in your System Folder. If you would like to try out a specific font, drag it to your closed System Folder. You should see a message stating that the fonts will be moved to the Fonts folder In the case of Type I fonts, you might need to drag multiple files to your System Folder.

Fonts (Windows)

Fonts should be installed by means of the Fonts Control Panel. Under Windows 95 or Windows NT 4.0 open Start Menu➡Settings➡Control Panel➡Fonts. Then select File➡Install New Font...from the File menu and select the font from the CD-ROM which you want to install. The fonts can all be found within the Fonts directory on the CD-ROM.

Stock imagery and textures

The stock photos and textures located in the Images folder do not need to be copied to your hard drive. Because many of them are very large, you'll want to open them from the CD-ROM so they do not take up all the space on your hard drive. For most files, you can double-click on them to open them in Photoshop. If they do not, try opening Photoshop first, then select File➡Open. Then choose the file you would like to open. If you particularly like a certain image and would like to access it quickly, by all means copy it to your hard drive.

A Note about Shareware

If you use any shareware items beyond an initial trial period, you are obligated to follow the guidelines set forth by the author; this is usually in the form of a reasonable shareware payment. Your purchase of this book and the accompanying CD-ROM does not release you from this obligation. Refer to the READ ME and other information files that accompany each of the programs for specifics.

Appendix B

Contributor's Listing

Fonts

Fonthead Design (Mac and PC)

1872-B Darryl Drive
Tallahassee, FL 32301-6017
ethan@fonthead.com
http://www.fonthead.com

Snyder Shareware Fonts (Mac and PC)

1797 Ross Inlet Road
Coos Bay, OR 97420
http://www.coos.or.us/~snyderrp/
snyderrp@mailF.coos.or.us   rps82@aol.com   76307.2431@compuserve.com

Synstelien Design (Mac and PC)

1338 North 120th Plaza Apt. # 9
Omaha, NE 68154
Phone: (402) 491-3065
http://www.synfonts.com
dsynstftrel@aol.com

Vintage Type (Mac and PC

5662 Calle Real #146
Goleta, CA 93117-2317
http://www.vintagetype.com/
sales@vintagetype.com

Effects

AutoFX Sample Edge Effects (Mac and PC)

15 North Main Street Suite 8
Wolfeboro, NH 03894
Phone: (603) 569-8800
Fax: (603) 569-9702
http://www.autofx.com
sales@autofx.com

Software & Filters

Adobe Systems, Inc.

345 Park Avenue
San Jose, CA 95110-6000
Phone: (408) 536-6000
Fax: (408) 537-6000
sales@adobe.com
http://www.adobe.com
On the CD-ROM:
Acrobat Reader 3.0 (Mac and PC)
Photoshop 3.0.5 Tryout (Mac and PC)
After Effects 3.0 Tryout (Mac only)
Streamline 3.1 Tryout (Mac and PC)
Dimensions 2.0 Tryout (Mac only)
Illustrator 6.0 Tryout (Mac only)

Alien Skin Software

1100 Wake Forest Rd. Suite 101
Raleigh, NC 27604
Phone: (919) 832-4124
Fax: (919) 832-4065
alien-skinfo@alienskin.com
http://www.alienskin.com
On the CD-ROM:
Eye Candy 3.0 Demo (Mac and PC)

Andromeda Software, Inc.

699 Hampshire Rd. Suite 109
Thousand Oaks, CA 91361
Phone: (800) 547-0055 or (805) 379-4109
Fax: (805) 379-5253
orders@andromeda.com
http://www.andromeda.com
On the CD-ROM:
Series 1, 2, & 3 Demos (Mac and PC)

Chris Cox

110 Oakland Circle
Madison, AL 35758-8663
ccox@teleport.com|
http://www.teleport.com/~ccox
On the CD-ROM:
Chris's Filters 3.0 (Mac only)

DataStream Imaging Systems, Inc.

P.O. Box 2148
Lexington, KY 40595-2148
(800) 889-7781 (Orders Only)
Phone: (606) 264-0302
Fax: (606) 263-0183
http://www.datastrem.com
ftp.datastrem.com
On the CD-ROM:
Wild River SSK Demo (Mac only)

Equilibrium

3 Harbor Drive Suite 111
Sausalito, CA 94965
Phone: (415) 332-4433
Fax: (415) 332-4433
BBS: (415) 332-6152
sales@equilibrium.com
http://www.equilibrium.com
On the CD-ROM:
DeBabelizer Pro Demo (Windows only)
DeBabelizer Lite LE (Mac only)
DeBabelizer 1.6.5 Demo (Mac only)

Jawai Interactive, Inc.

401 East Fourth Street Suite 443
Austin, TX 78701-3745
Phone: (800) 600-6706 or (512) 469-0502
Fax: (512) 469-7850
info@jawai.com
http://www.jawai.com
On the CD-ROM:
ScreenCaffeine Demo (Mac and PC)

MetaTools, Inc.

6303 Carpinteria Ave.
Carpinteria, CA 93013
(805) 566-6200
metasales@aol.com
http://www.metatools.com
Neil Schulman
nwcs@usit.net
On the CD-ROM:
KPT 3.0 Demo (Mac and PC)
Frosty Filter (Mac only)

247

Specular, International

7 Pomeroy Lane
Amherst, MA 01002
Phone: (800) 433-SPEC
Fax: (413) 253-0540
sales@specular.com
http://www.specular.com
On the CD-ROM:
Infini-D Demo (Mac and PC)
Collage 2.0 Demo (Mac only)
LogoMotion Demo (Mac only)
TextureScape Demo (Mac only)

Xaos Tools, Inc.

55 Hawthorn Suite 1000
San Francisco, CA 94105
Phone: (800) BUY-XAOS
macinfo@xaostools.com
http://www.xaostools.com
On the CD-ROM:
Paint Alchemy 2 Demo (Mac only)
Terrazo 2 Demo (Mac only)
TypeCaster Demo (Mac only)

Stock Images
Digital Stock

400 S. Sierra Ave., Suite 100
Solana Beach, CA 92075
Phone: (619) 794-4040 or (800) 545-4514
Fax: (619) 794-4041
http://www.digitalstock.com
sales@digitalstock.com

D'Pix Division of Amber Productions, Inc.

414 W. Fourth Ave.
Columbus, OH 43201
Phone: (614) 299-7192
Fax: (614) 294-0002

FotoSets

4104 24th St., #425
San Francisco, CA 94114
Phone: (415) 621-2061
Fax: (415) 621-2917

Image Club Graphics

729 24th Ave. SE
Calgary, AB Canada
T2G 5K8
Phone: (403) 262-8008 or (800) 661-9410
Fax: (403)261-7013
http://www.adobe.com/imageclub

Photo24 Texture Resource

7948 Faust Ave.
West Hills, CA 91304
Phone: (818) 999-4184 or (800) 582-9492 (outside CA)
Fax: (818) 999-5704
http://www.photo24.com

PhotoDisc/CMCD

2013 Fourth Ave., 4th Floor
Seattle, WA 98121
Phone: (206) 441-9355 or (800) 528-3472
http://www.photodisc.com

Gallery

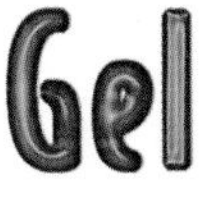

page 86

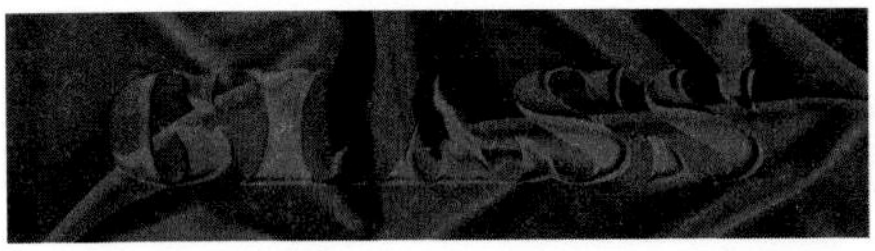

page 90

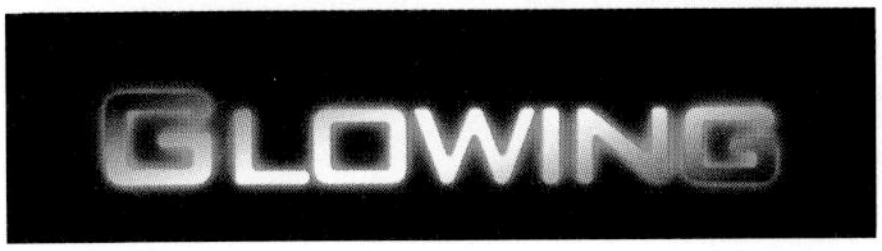

page 96

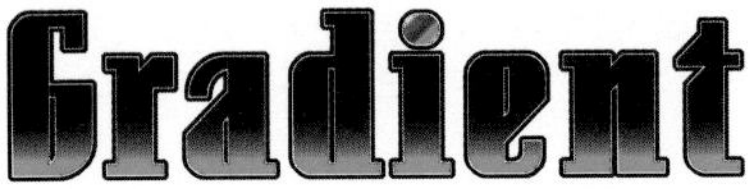

page 104

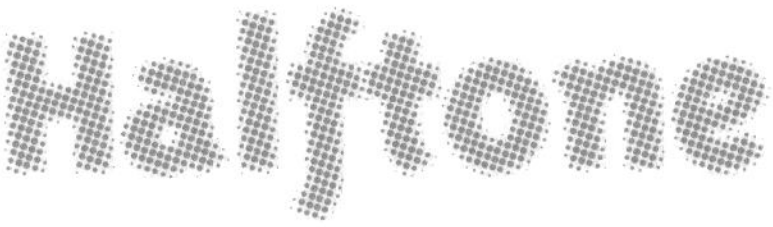

page 110

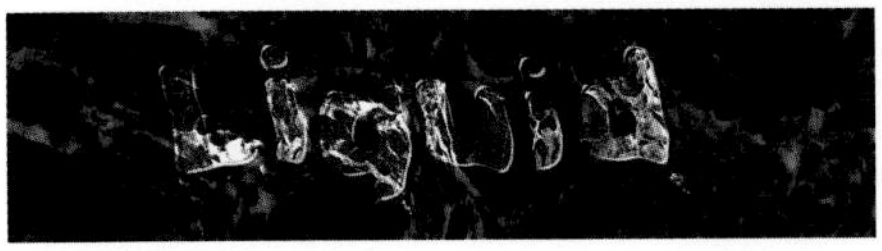

page 116

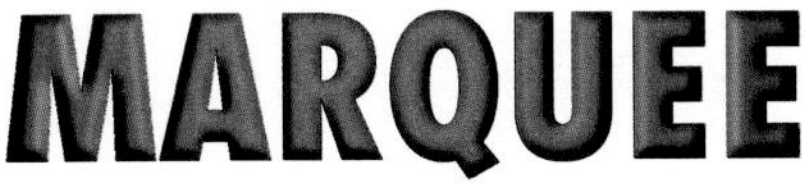

page 124

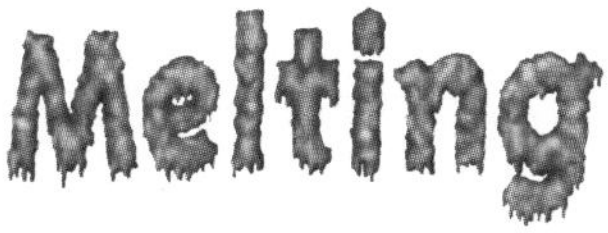

page 126

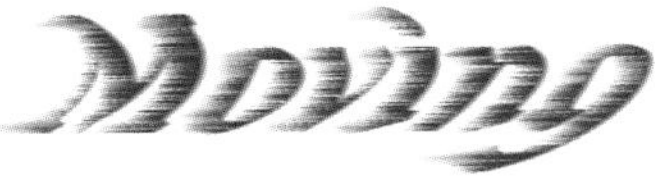

page 130

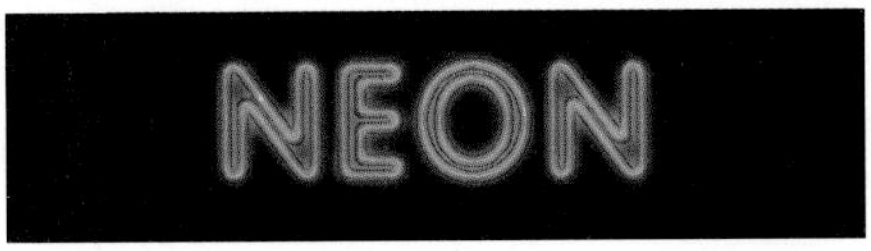

page 134

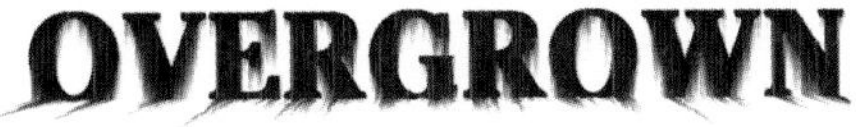

page 142

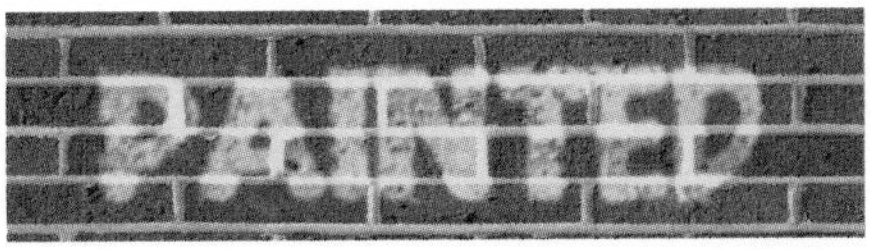

page 148

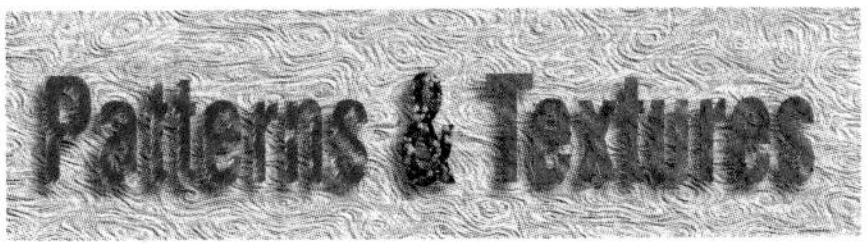

page 154

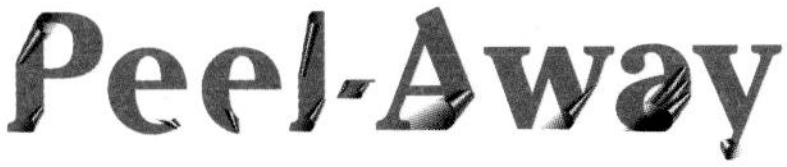

page 160

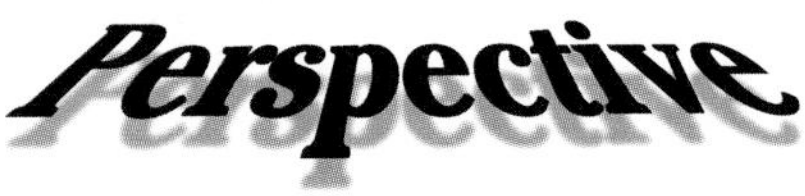

page 166

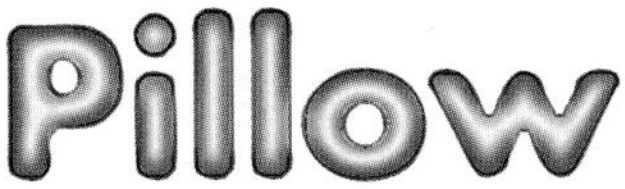

page 170

MACMILLAN COMPUTER PUBLISHING USA

A **VIACOM** COMPANY

Technical ---- Support:

If you cannot get the CD/Disk to install properly, or you need assistance with a particular situation in the book, please feel free to check out the Knowledge Base on our Web site at **http://www.superlibrary.com/general/support**. We have answers to our most Frequently Asked Questions listed there. If you do not find your specific question answered, please contact Macmillan Technical Support at **(317) 581-3833**. We can also be reached by email at **support@mcp.com**.